A Disciple's Journey

A Disciple's Journey

*26 Devotional Studies
to Draw You Closer to Jesus*

John T. Leach

XULON PRESS

Xulon Press
2301 Lucien Way #415
Maitland, FL 32751
407.339.4217
www.xulonpress.com

© 2019 by John T. Leach

All rights reserved solely by the author. The author guarantees all contents are original and do not infringe upon the legal rights of any other person or work. No part of this book may be reproduced in any form without the permission of the author. The views expressed in this book are not necessarily those of the publisher.

1. All scripture quotations, unless otherwise indicated, are taken from the NEW KING JAMES VERSION® (NKJV). Copyright© 1982 by Thomas Nelson, Inc. Used by permission. All rights reserved.
2. Scriptures marked NIV are taken from THE HOLY BIBLE, NEW INTERNATIONAL VERSION ®. Copyright© 1973, 1978, 1984, 2011 by Biblica, Inc.™. Used by permission of Zondervan
3. Scriptures marked KJV are taken from the KING JAMES VERSION (KJV), public domain.
4. Scriptures marked TPT are from The Passion Translation (TPT) ®. Copyright © 2017, 2018 by Passion & Fire Ministries, Inc. Used by permission. All rights reserved. ThePassionTranslation.com.
5. Scriptures marked ESV are taken from THE HOLY BIBLE, ENGLISH STANDARD VERSION (ESV) ® Copyright© 2001 by Crossway, a publishing ministry of Good News Publishers. Used by permission.
6. Scriptures marked NLT are taken from the HOLY BIBLE, NEW LIVING TRANSLATION (NLT), Copyright© 1996, 2004, 2007 by Tyndale House Foundation. Used by permission of Tyndale House Publishers, Inc., Carol Stream, Illinois 60188. All rights reserved. Used by permission.
7. Scriptures marked ISV are taken from INTERNATIONAL STANDARD VERSION (ISV), copyright© 1996-2008 by the ISV Foundation. All rights reserved internationally.
8. Scriptures marked BSB are taken from The Holy Bible, Berean Study Bible, BSB Copyright ©2016, 2018 by Bible Hub. Used by Permission. All Rights Reserved Worldwide.
9. Scriptures marked HCSB are taken from the HOLMAN CHRISTIAN STANDARD BIBLE (HCSB), copyright© 1999, 2000, 2002, 2003 by Holman Bible Publishers, Nashville Tennessee. All rights reserved.
10. Hymn: How Firm a Foundation, Ye Saints of the Lord (Anonymous/Unknown, published 1787, Public Domain)
11. My Utmost for His Highest by Oswald Chambers, copyright© 1935, by Dodd, Mead & Company, Inc. Copyright renewed 1963 by Oswald Chambers Publications Association, Ltd. Permission not needed for small quotation
12. Every Man's Battle, Copyright© 2000, by Stephen Arterburn, Fred Stoeker, and Mike Yorkey. Used by permission.

The photo of the lake at sundown was taken by the author or his wife and is used by permission. All other photos are used by permission through Pixabay where no attribution is required.

Printed in the United States of America.

ISBN-13: 978-1-6305-0236-2

What Others Are Saying About *A Disciple's Journey*

As a young, on-staff minister I asked my senior pastor how I could best accelerate my walk with the Lord. At that time he suggested different authors with different strengths that I should study separately to increase my understanding of the different aspects of my walk with Jesus. John Leach has written a concise, yet comprehensive manual in one volume that answers the questions I asked of my pastor years ago. It arms us with the tools of the Scriptures that I have found to be most helpful in each stage of my life. He also tells us of the obstacles we will encounter along the way. He encourages us that Jesus will bring us through every trial. A strong practical life-changing book.

Fred Patete (Myrtle Beach, South Carolina)

Outstanding devotional! John Leach is a gifted writer who understands God's heart. I love how he personalizes the Gospel to our relationship to the Father. Here it is the reader searching his heart to find out what is important in his or her life and what the priorities are in their life. There is very little teaching today on becoming a disciple, unfortunately, and even less on the cost of being one. His book will go a long way in correcting that problem. I love the questions he asks. They make you think and examine your own life.

SweetPeaBuddy ("Paco")
Christian Leader and Devotional Writer on Chess.com

VERY good work! This could be used as a guideline for spiritual growth step by step.

wsswan (Sam–USA)
Seasoned prayer-warrior on Chess.com

Very well done. I can just imagine how many lives this will touch.

LHCSaraB (Sara–USA)
On-fire young Christian on Chess.com

Se ve que será un libro de mucha bendición.
Translation: You can see it will be a book of great blessing.

perrodelhoyo (David De Las Heras Saldaña–Mexico)
Evangelist on Chess.com

Dedication

Then the eleven disciples went to Galilee, to the mountain where Jesus had told them to go. When they saw him, they worshiped him; but some doubted. Then Jesus came to them and said, "All authority in heaven and on earth has been given to me. Therefore go and make disciples of all nations, baptizing them in the name of the Father and of the Son and of the Holy Spirit, and teaching them to obey everything I have commanded you. And surely I am with you always, to the very end of the age." Matthew 28:16-20 (NIV)

This book is dedicated to all those who have gone before me and helped me on my journey. It is also dedicated to those who will follow and spread the Word to others as they continue on their own journey as disciples of our Lord Jesus Christ. My prayer and hope are that God will use this book in some small way to help us fulfill His Great Commission.

"Becoming more like Jesus through Praying, Studying, Meditating, and Doing"

"Enter by the narrow gate; for wide is the gate and broad is the way that leads to destruction, and there are many who go in by it. Because narrow is the gate and difficult is the way which leads to life, and there are few who find it." Matthew 7:13-14

Table of Contents

Dedication.. vii
Introduction.. xiii
How to Track Your Progress xix

Are You Ready for the Journey?........................... 1
1. What Does God Really Want?............................... 3
   Pray, Study, Meditate, and Do - Chapter 1................. 8
2. The Goal: How to Enjoy a Fulfilling Relationship with God .. 10
   Pray, Study, Meditate, and Do - Chapter 2................ 16
3. Where Do You Start? With a Manger in Your Heart!........ 19
   Pray, Study, Meditate, and Do - Chapter 3................ 23

The Heart of the Problem Is the Problem of the Heart... 27
4. Who Is the Prodigal?..................................... 29
   Pray, Study, Meditate, and Do - Chapter 4................ 38
5. Fence Straddlers 42
   Pray, Study, Meditate, and Do - Chapter 5................ 47
6. Circumcising our Hearts 50
   Pray, Study, Meditate, and Do - Chapter 6................ 54
7. Let God Be Your Heart Surgeon 56
   Pray, Study, Meditate, and Do - Chapter 7................ 60

Overcoming Our Worldly Culture......................... 63
8. Living in a Moral Free-fall 65
   Pray, Study, Meditate, and Do - Chapter 8................ 71

9. Bubble Realities 74
   Pray, Study, Meditate, and Do - Chapter 9.................... 77
10. Overcoming Distractions and Goal Setting................. 79
   Pray, Study, Meditate, and Do - Chapter 10................... 85
11. Passive Adam or Proactive Jesus?........................... 88
   Pray, Study, Meditate, and Do - Chapter 11................... 92
12. We Each Need a Vision of God to Endure 96
   Pray, Study, Meditate, and Do - Chapter 12.................. 100

Overcoming Resistance from the Dark Side 105
13. Recognizing Your Enemies 107
   Pray, Study, Meditate, and Do - Chapter 13.................. 113
14. How to Fight the Good Fight and Overcome Your Enemies 118
   Pray, Study, Meditate, and Do - Chapter 14.................. 124

Overcoming the Pull of the Flesh 129
15. Your Focus Factor 131
   Pray, Study, Meditate, and Do - Chapter 15.................. 136
16. The Importance of Discipline............................. 139
   Pray, Study, Meditate, and Do - Chapter 16.................. 144
17. Overcoming Inertia and Goal Setting 147
   Pray, Study, Meditate, and Do - Chapter 17.................. 151
18. Maintaining Your Balance 154
   Pray, Study, Meditate, and Do - Chapter 18.................. 158

Help from High Places 161
19. God's Law and Grace...................................... 163
   Pray, Study, Meditate, and Do - Chapter 19.................. 174
20. Checking Your Progress through the Beatitudes 179
   Pray, Study, Meditate, and Do - Chapter 20.................. 186
21. Your Pearl of Great Price 191
   Pray, Study, Meditate, and Do - Chapter 21.................. 194
22. Your Valley of Dry Bones 197
   Pray, Study, Meditate, and Do - Chapter 22.................. 201

Destined to Reign with the King 205
23. A Bride for the King 207
    Pray, Study, Meditate, and Do - Chapter 23 214
24. Ruling with Jesus 217
    Pray, Study, Meditate, and Do - Chapter 24 221
25. Conclusion: He Is Worth It and so Are You! 224
    Pray, Study, Meditate, and Do - Chapter 25 228

Looking Back and Moving Forward 231
26. Rejoicing in your Progress and Suggestions For
    Moving Forward 233
    Pray, Study, Meditate, and Do - Chapter 26 236

Appendix 241
    How I Became a Christian 242

Introduction

For this is the love of God, that we keep His commandments. And His commandments are not burdensome.
1 John 5:3

This book is about the journey of a disciple of Jesus Christ. It is about my journey and may also be about yours if you seek to follow Jesus after receiving Him as Savior. Although our paths won't be identical, there will be similarities. This book came into being because I sensed the Lord wanted me to share some things I have learned along the way and continue to relearn because they may help you on your journey. We all have the same destination: to become more like Jesus and to be drawn closer to His heart. If you want to find out more about how I began my journey or how you can begin yours, I invite you to read *How I Became a Christian* in the appendix.

Before we begin our journey, we must realize no matter how well-intentioned, our own efforts cannot bridge the gap that separates us from God. God draws us to Himself and offers the gift of faith in Christ as we trust in Him and His finished work on the cross. Then He gives us a new life that pleases Him. We share in the resurrection life of Jesus Christ and leave our old life behind. As we enter into this new life, we learn to walk by faith depending on God to lead and empower us. When we walk in union with Christ, trusting Him, obeying God is not difficult. Our challenge is to get to the point where we completely trust Him in all that we do.

To the natural mind, the true Christian life makes no sense. It is not burdensome (1 John 5:3) but without God, it is impossible (John 3:5-6). Because Jesus paid it all, it costs us nothing (John 3:16). But following Jesus will require us to lay down the lives we once had and surrender control of our lives to Him (Luke 14:25-33). When we give our lives to Jesus, He gives us so much more than what we left behind (Matthew 19:27-29).

The problem is we do not want to let go of what we have to possess what we do not see and cannot control. It is like trying to take a bone out of the mouth of a hungry bulldog. You do it at your own risk! The best way is to offer him a nice juicy steak. Then he will gladly let go of that old bone. Our natural mind does not see that nice juicy steak of a new life in Christ. We must perceive it by faith. The natural man wants to hold on to that old life, like the bulldog with only a bone. The Christian life makes no sense to the natural man.

Because of the nature of life and its trials, and the testing of our faith with its setbacks, there is no easy road to Christian maturity. It doesn't just happen. Salvation is a gift but becoming a disciple requires surrendering to Jesus. The process of surrendering does not happen all at once but is usually done in small incremental steps as we learn to trust Jesus incrementally. He promises to give us grace as we need it so we can pass through the trials successfully. Without having a faith-vision, we are like that old bulldog and just want to hang on to what we have. Growing as a Christian goes hand-in-hand with renewing our minds, a process necessary for maturity.

Introduction

A disciple must be willing to deny himself, take up his cross daily, and follow Jesus (Matthew 16:24). Those who respond to the call will find He is more than they had ever dreamed. Those who persevere in following Jesus and overcome through God's grace will find the reward is well worth the cost. I hope you are among them. If so, *A Disciple's Journey* was designed with you in mind to help you along the way. You can return to it any time you want to be refreshed in its concepts or motivated to develop additional godly habits.

Welcome to *Volume I* of *A Disciple's Journey: 26 Devotional Studies to Draw You Closer to Jesus*. We are each on our own journey with God. There are signposts along the way to help guide us and let us know we are on the right path to Christian maturity. We will be deepening our personal walk with the Lord and interacting with other Christians as we take up the Great Commission (Matthew 28:18-20). This book provides help to understand and overcome the challenges we will all face. It will not replace one-on-one or small group discipleship and assumes a basic knowledge of the Bible. *Volume I* focuses more on your personal walk with the Lord and can be done individually or in a group setting. *Volume II* will focus more on one-on-one and small group discipleship.

This book does not provide a course in systematic theology or a complete foundation for the Christian life. However, it does address foundational areas for discipleship in an interactive way. *A Disciple's Journey* was designed to help you partner with the Lord to build and strengthen character qualities that move you closer to Him. I hope you find the devotional studies both inspiring and enlightening. They have come through a life of many ups and downs from someone first introduced to the Lord almost fifty years ago.

There are different ways of approaching these devotional studies. Some may benefit by first reading the devotionals to get an overview and then returning to do the studies at a pace and order of their own choosing.

Those who benefit the most will have read the devotionals, answered the questions, and formed new habits. Ideally, they will have formed twenty-six new habits to celebrate as they progress along the road to Christian maturity. Others will be successful in forming a few new habits that draw them closer to Jesus. If you continue on the journey, you have not failed regardless of your level of success. Then we can celebrate our success together!

Experts say it takes twenty-one days to establish a habit. *A Disciple's Journey* was designed with this in mind. Each volume contains twenty-six devotionals with the corresponding *Pray, Study, Meditate, and Do* sections and is designed to be completed in a year. Doing the devotional studies without developing new character habits can be done in much less time and should be beneficial but would defeat their primary purpose.

Each study is designed to take two weeks and may require an average of half an hour or more per day to complete with excellence. The first week can be used for reading the devotional; interacting with the Lord through prayer and meditation; answering the questions where Scripture references are provided; identifying the change to make into a new habit, and continuing to form the habit identified in the previous devotional. During the second week, you should focus on developing the new habit while establishing the previous one. You will also delve deeper into the subject of the devotional through answering questions that require researching the Scriptures on your own.

Doing the research questions should increase your understanding and deepen your foundation. As you see the importance of these character qualities, it should strengthen your resolve for developing them. Seeking the Lord to identify and establish desirable character qualities while partnering with Him is essential. Remember, depending on the Lord's strength and following His leading is the key to discipleship.

INTRODUCTION

There are 323 exercises, some with multiple questions. Answers will be personalized and some may require several paragraphs. Recording your answers and tracking your progress in making the desired character changes will ensure you get the most benefit from these studies. See *How to Track Your Progress* in the next section for a suggestion. I also recommend recording your answers electronically or in a notebook since sufficient space is not provided here. You can explore the recommended resources that interest you at any time.

Each godly character trait you turn into a habit brings you one step closer to Jesus.

How to Track Your Progress

Therefore, my dear friends, as you have always obeyed—not only in my presence, but now much more in my absence—continue to work out your salvation with fear and trembling, for it is God who works in you to will and to act in order to fulfill his good purpose. Philippians 2:12-13 (NIV)

WARNING: Making progress in forming good habits can be habit-forming! One simple way of tracking your progress is through using a standard calendar. You will only use the "Sunday" and "Saturday" columns. Use "Sunday" to mark the week you began the new habit and "Saturday" to mark the week it was established, twenty-one days later. Begin by marking a "1" in the "Sunday" box the week after you plan to start the course. This shows when you begin to form your first new habit. Then skip a week and mark a "2" in the "Sunday" box to show when you begin to form your second habit. Then mark a "1" in the "Saturday" box for that week to show when your first habit was established. Continue in this pattern, skipping every other week, as indicated in the matrix below. Continue using this pattern until you have indicated the start and end week for all twenty-six habits.

Sunday	Week	you	started	the	course	Saturday
1-start ☺	☺	☺	☺	☺	☺	☺
☺	☺	☺	☺	☺	☺	☺
2-start ☺ ☺	☺ ☺	☺ ☺	☺ ☺	☺ ☺	☺ ☺	1-finish ☺ ☺
☺	☺	☺	☺	☺	☺	☺
3-start ☺	☺ ☺	☺ ☺	☺ ☺	☺ ☺	☺ ☺	2-finish ☺ ☺
☺	☺	☺	☺	☺	☺	☺
4-start	☺ ☺	☺ ☺	☺ ☺	☺ ☺	☺ ☺	3-finish ☺ ☺
☺	☺	☺	☺	☺	☺	☺

To encourage yourself, you could draw a smiley face in the date box of the calendar for any day you successfully followed your new habit (see matrix above). On days when you are starting one new habit and establishing the previous one, you could add a smiley face for each habit you successfully followed. The matrix above indicates the person was almost 100% successful in practicing their new habits, just missing perfection on a couple of Sundays. When you successfully formed a habit after twenty-one days, keep track of it in your private notebook by writing down the habit formed, its number, and the date you finished. Trust me! You'll be glad you did!

If you experience failure, do not let that discourage you. We all experience failure. It is what you do after you failed that is the most important thing. Do you confess your sin to the Lord and believe He has cleansed you (1 John 1:9)? Do you go on with your walk with the Lord and your commitment to follow Him? Remember we all fall down many times. We fall down and get up. We fall down and get up. We fall down and get up…

> ***Though a righteous man falls seven times, he will get up.***
> (Proverbs 24:16a; HCSB)

May you persevere on your journey as a disciple of Jesus Christ.

My hope is that *A Disciple's Journey* will help you along the way.

Are You Ready for the Journey?

Chapters 1-3

Grace has commonly been defined as *unmerited favor* or through the acrostic, **God's Riches At Christ's Expense**. I like to think of grace as *Christ-merited favor*. Christ-merited favor is what Jesus Christ deserves. It is given to us as a gift through faith in Him. *Faith* in this context can be defined as confidence in God, His character, His Word, and His promises. It is more than mere head knowledge and lodges in the heart, producing action based on that confidence. Such faith is a gift of God and not something produced by man's efforts or desires. Grace is what God has made available to us in Christ and faith appropriates it for our use.

To succeed in the Christian life requires a deep understanding and application of grace and a persevering faith that grows deeper through the trials of life. Trials are designed by God to test our faith and help us mature (1 Peter 4:13; James 1:2-3). God will enable His saints to persevere through trials without abandoning their faith (see 2 Timothy 1:12). Your faith and perseverance will be tested as you work your way through these devotional studies both by the studies themselves and by the events that transpire in your life. God has given you the overcoming life of Jesus Christ. If you keep your eyes, mind, and heart focused on Him, you will endure to the end and bring Him great joy.

These devotional studies provide insight into different aspects of the Christian life. By partnering with God through studying His Word and yielding to His Spirit, you will become more like Christ. Expect some resistance and some pain along the way. Old habits are hard to break and the enemy will resist you in establishing godly habits. God will help you break bad habits and replace them with good ones. After taking twenty-one days to form a good habit, it will take some effort to maintain it. You will need discipline and diligence to succeed but God is your Helper and Christ in you is the One who overcomes.

Enjoy the journey!

"Commit your work to the LORD, and your plans will be established." (Proverbs 16:3; ESV)

1

WHAT DOES GOD REALLY WANT?

After removing Saul, he made David their king. God testified concerning him: "I have found David son of Jesse, a man after my own heart; he will do everything I want him to do." Acts 13:22 (NIV)

We all want something out of life but we do not always know what we really want. Our priorities and desires can change as well as our awareness of them. Do you know what your "top ten" desires are? How about your top three or your number one desire? The answers to these questions may not be obvious. You may want to take some time to reflect and write down what you discover about your own heart and what your chief desires are. Similarly, we may think we know what God wants but it may not be what He really wants.

God created us and promises to give us the desires of our hearts if we delight in Him (Psalm 37:4). The Creator of our hearts also has a heart. Have you ever wondered what the chief or greatest desire of God's heart is? That's what this devotional study is about: what God really wants as His number one desire.

Arguably the best-known verse in the Bible is John 3:16. It may also be the most loved verse. John 3:16 says, "For God so loved the world that He gave His only begotten Son, that whoever believes in Him should not perish but have everlasting life." The Holy Bible reveals the greatest desire of God's heart is for us to be reconciled to Him. He is a good God and He loves us. He called Jesus His "beloved Son" yet He gave Him up for us. He wants us to be reconciled to Him and share everlasting life with Him.

But what is *everlasting life*? Does it simply mean to live forever? Does it mean to live forever with God or does it mean something else? Jesus answers this question in John 17:3: "Now this is eternal life: that they may know You, the only true God, and Jesus Christ, whom You have sent." *Eternal life* means to know the only true God and Jesus Christ.

We can know what God and others have revealed about themselves. But knowing someone can mean many different things. It certainly means more than knowing about them. We can know about others through what we read or hear about them. We can assess what they have done and draw our own conclusions. But we don't have direct access to their hearts. God revealed the greatest desire of His heart through sending His Son to die on the cross for us so that we might know Him (John 3:16). God then gives us access to His heart through His Word and by His Spirit that we might know Him intimately (1 Corinthians 2:1-16).

Jesus continues in John 17:25-26, "O righteous Father! The world has not known You, but I have known You; and these have known that You sent Me. And I have declared to them Your name, and will declare it, that the love with which You loved Me may be in them, and I in them." Jesus also said, "protect them by the power of your name, the name you gave me, so they may be one as we are one" (John 17:11b; NIV). John 17 gives us the answer to what God really wants through Jesus's great priestly intercessory prayer. God's greatest desire is for us to know Him and become one with Him.

God created us for Him but He didn't create us to be robots. He gave each of us a will, a mind, and a heart. He wants us to enter into a voluntary oneness with the Father, the Son, and the Holy Spirit. He will not force it upon us but will work in our hearts so we desire it. He wants the greatest desire of our hearts to match His: to choose Him and to become one with Him. When He has our hearts, our deepest fulfillment will be realized and we will be at rest in Him. But what hinders this from happening?

First, let us consider what cannot separate us from God's love. Romans 8:35-39 provides a short list.

> *Who shall separate us from the love of Christ? Shall tribulation, or distress, or persecution, or famine, or nakedness, or peril, or sword? As it is written:*
>
> *"For Your sake we are killed all day long;*
> *We are accounted as sheep for the slaughter."*
>
> *Yet in all these things we are more than conquerors through Him who loved us. For I am persuaded that neither death nor life, nor angels nor principalities nor powers, nor things present nor things to come, nor height nor depth, nor any other created thing, shall be able to separate us from the love of God which is in Christ Jesus our Lord.*

There is one and only one thing that keeps us from knowing God and from entering into union with Him. It is our sin. As Isaiah 59: 1-3 says,

"Behold, the LORD's hand is not shortened, that it cannot save; nor His ear heavy, that it cannot hear. But your iniquities have separated you from your God; and your sins have hidden *His* face from you, so that He will not hear. For your hands are defiled with blood, and your fingers with iniquity; your lips have spoken lies, your tongue has muttered perversity."

Jesus removed that barrier through His death on the cross. He reconciles us to God when we receive Him. But if we walk in darkness our sin blocks our fellowship with God (1 John 1:6-7) even though we may still have a relationship with Him. When we love God, we willingly follow Him. He will not dominate us and compel us to obey Him through fear, intimidation, guilt, or duty.

Sin is more than doing what is morally wrong or failing to do what is morally right. The essence of sin is having a will set at odds with God and His will. We usually want to manage and control our own lives. We do not like others to tell us what to do or to dictate how we are to live. We resist submitting to someone who wants to dominate us. But God's will is for us to know and become one with Him which requires us to submit to Him. To do this we must first know true freedom and fulfillment come only to those who are willing to submit to Him and to be freed from the tyranny of "self." But we seem to think we can do a better job than God because we want to run our own lives. God will allow or engineer circumstances in our lives to break us of our self-centered wills so that we are willing to follow Him.

Even when we know we need help in managing our lives, we are reluctant to trust someone else. Too often we have been let down. Too often we have been hurt because we have trusted someone else and they have let us down. With good reason, we are not ready to entrust someone else with our lives. But can we trust God and His wisdom? Can we relinquish all control over our lives to God and trust Him to lead us into what is best? Are we willing to trust Him and allow Him to choose for us?

How can we trust God if we do not know Him? And how can we know Him if we do not trust Him? This is another form of the old dilemma: "Which came first: the chicken or the egg?" As we perceive God's love (Romans 5:8; 1 John 4:19), we learn to trust and love Him. Our love for God compels us to obey Him (2 Corinthians 5:14). As we trust and obey God, He continues to reveal Himself and His love. Love, trust, and obedience are linked together with knowing God.

God knows our dilemma and He is willing to meet us where we are. When we come to Him, we are like a newborn baby. He knows we have to learn how to sit before we can stand and stand before we can walk. He also knows the progression of taking baby steps comes before walking with confidence and that walking comes before running. He also knows how to build endurance in us so we can run in a marathon race. Life is like a marathon and God wants us to be free to run with Him. To get there, we need to take things incrementally, starting at where we are now.

As we gradually discover that God is different from others and is trustworthy, we will grow in our willingness and ability to trust Him. Our love for God and trust in Him will grow together. These qualities are displayed to the degree that we learn to obey Him. Our love and trust will grow step-by-step as one act of obedience follows another.

Eventually, we can learn how to habitually obey God and that's a very good thing! We are truly free when we go with God, obeying Him through easy and difficult situations. He is a patient Father and a good Father. He will continue to work with us to help us get to where He knows we need to go.

God wants us to love Him with all that we are and to trust Him fully. He wants us to become one with Him as Jesus prayed in John 17. He calls us into a holy oneness with the Trinity: the Father, the Son, and the Holy Spirit. God really wants us to enjoy this kind of intimacy with Him. As Jesus said, eternal life is for us to know God and Jesus Christ Whom He has sent (John 17:3).

Chapter 1 – What Does God Really Want?

Pray, Study, Meditate, and Do

Key Scripture: *After removing Saul, he made David their king. God testified concerning him: "I have found David son of Jesse, a man after my own heart; he will do everything I want him to do."* Acts 13:22 (NIV)

Ask God to help you as you work through this devotional study. Feel free to add to or change your answers any time. You are encouraged to write all your answers.

1. During this week take some time to search your heart before God and discover your greatest desires.
2. Can you identify your top ten desires? Write as many of them down as you can.
3. Can you identify your top three desires? If so, write them down.
4. Can you identify your greatest desire? If so, write it down.
5. Consider these Bible passages. What do they tell you about some of the desires of God's heart? Psalm 37:4, Ezekiel 18:32,

Hebrews 11:6, Matthew 22: 36-40. Identify and write down God's desires as expressed in each passage.
6. Use an Internet search engine or a concordance if necessary and find some other Bible passages that show desires in the heart of God. Write down the references and identify what desires of God's heart they identify.
7. Try to find Bible passages to identify ten of the top desires of God's heart. Write the references down and what desires they point to.
8. How do your top desires compare with God's top desires for you?
9. Ask God to purify your heart to align your will and desires more closely with His. Look for Him to show you what you can do to cooperate with Him as He purifies your heart.
10. Ask God to show you a few things you can do to help move your heart toward His heart for you. Write these things down.
11. Choose one of the things God has shown you and work on making it into a habit and incorporating it into your life. Input it into your mobile device or write it on a 3" by 5" index card and carry it with you. Review it several times a day. See how you do and chart your progress.

Recommended resources and/or projects for those who want to go deeper: *Shattered Dreams God's Unexpected Path to Joy* by Dr. Larry Crabb

2

THE GOAL: HOW TO ENJOY A FULFILLING RELATIONSHIP WITH GOD

There they made Him a supper; and Martha served, but Lazarus was one of those who sat at the table with Him. Then Mary took a pound of very costly oil of spikenard, anointed the feet of Jesus, and wiped His feet with her hair. And the house was filled with the fragrance of the oil. John 12:2-3

Before we can know how to enjoy a fulfilling relationship with God it is good to ask these two questions: Where do I get my greatest fulfillment in life? What do I think will bring me even greater fulfillment? Understanding why God created us is a great place to start our search for these answers.

As we open our Bibles we find some answers in the first chapter of Genesis. God reveals how he designed man and defines the scope of his responsibilities.

> *Then God said, "Let Us make man in Our image, according to Our likeness; let them have dominion over the fish of the sea, over the birds of the air, and over the cattle, over all the earth and over every creeping thing that creeps on the earth." So God created man in His own image; in the image of God He created him; male and female He created them. Then God blessed them, and God said to them, "Be fruitful and multiply; fill the earth and subdue it; have dominion over the fish of the sea, over the birds of the air, and over every living thing that moves on the earth." (Genesis 1:26-28)*

This passage reveals God created us for a very special purpose, to be His image-bearers. We were made to rule and subdue but not rule over and subdue each other. We were created to have relationships with God and with each other. Without God's blessing we cannot do what we were designed to do and fulfill God's purpose for our lives.

Because of Adam's and Eve's disobedience, man's direct relationship with God was lost and he was brought under a curse. Even then God had a plan to restore our relationship with Him and made it possible by sending His Son to die for our sins. Receiving Jesus as Savior and trusting Him as Lord gives us a new life and a restored relationship with God. God gives us a new heart and eternal life so we may know and love Him supremely. Through this new life, we can also love our neighbor as ourselves. I believe God, in His wisdom, knew our greatest fulfillment would only come from having an intimate loving relationship with Him. When we love, trust, and obey God we draw closer to Him.

Having a fulfilling relationship with God through Jesus Christ has many different dimensions. Three of the most important aspects are wonderfully illustrated in the relationships Jesus had with His friends Mary, Martha, and Lazarus. This will be the focus of our devotional study.

You may recall Mary, Martha, and Lazarus were siblings. They lived together and were close friends of Jesus. Scripture records a time when Jesus went to dine with Mary and Martha.

> *Now it happened as they went He entered a certain village; and a certain woman named Martha welcomed Him into her house. And she had a sister called Mary, who also sat at Jesus's feet and heard His word. But Martha was distracted with much serving, and she approached Him and said, "Lord, do You not care that my sister has left me to serve alone? Therefore tell her to help me."*
>
> *And Jesus answered and said to her, "Martha, Martha, you are worried and troubled about many things. But one thing is needed, and Mary has chosen that good part, which will not be taken away from her."* (Luke 10:38-42)

I'm sure we can all relate to Martha when we have more on our plate than we know how to handle. Martha was stressed out and asked Jesus to release her sister to help. But Mary was occupied while she was sitting at the feet of Jesus, soaking in His presence, and intently listening to His every word. Martha was probably caught off guard when Jesus delivered a gentle rebuke, explaining Mary had chosen the better part.

For Jesus, some things were more important than having a special meal together. He preferred spending quality time with Mary who wanted to know Him better and rest in His presence. To listen attentively to Him, she had to block out all distractions. Are we willing to do this and spent quality time with Jesus to please Him? When you find yourself very busy and getting stressed out, why not ask Jesus if you are doing what He wants? If not, maybe you need to readjust your priorities to have a closer relationship with Him.

Mary illustrated the first and most important aspect of a fulfilling relationship with Jesus. She shows us what it means to worship Jesus through being attentive to Him and His Word while soaking in His presence. Cultivating an attitude of worship in this manner is of utmost importance to Jesus. If you can do only one thing, this is what you should do. To enter into His rest, we must cease from our own labors. We can be at peace even when those closest to us get overloaded and seek our help to complete their self-assigned projects. Can we ignore the pleas of our loved ones so we can draw closer to Jesus? Will we give Him uninterrupted time to develop an intimate relationship with Him? If we are close to Jesus, He will let us know when to leave the quiet place to help someone else.

Those who worship the Lord are not exempt from challenging circumstances. Mary's and Martha's faith was severely tested through the death of their brother, Lazarus. Jesus knew the grief and pain Mary and Martha were experiencing. He did not save his friend, Lazarus, from dying but He wept at his funeral. Mary and Martha did not know it was God's will to allow Lazarus to die. Nor did they know Lazarus' death was the opportunity for God to bring great glory to Himself through Jesus raising him from the dead. You can read the full account in the eleventh chapter of John, verses 5-43.

When traumatic events like these disrupt our personal world, life becomes very hard. It is impossible for us in our own strength to keep our focus on the Lord through reverential worship. If we take the time to develop intimacy with the Lord in our daily walk, He will provide the resources to weather our personal traumas and storms. He may provide special grace through His manifest presence, prayer, and the loving presence and acts of family and friends.

Let's look at another time where Jesus interacted with these special friends.

> *Then, six days before the Passover, Jesus came to Bethany, where Lazarus was who had been dead, whom He had raised from the dead. There they made Him a supper; and Martha served, but Lazarus was one of those who sat at the table with Him. Then Mary took a pound of very costly oil of spikenard, anointed the feet of Jesus, and wiped His feet with her hair. And the house was filled with the fragrance of the oil.*
>
> *But one of His disciples, Judas Iscariot, Simon's son, who would betray Him, said, "Why was this fragrant oil not sold for three hundred denarii and given to the poor?" This he said, not that he cared for the poor, but because he was a thief, and had the money box; and he used to take what was put in it.*
>
> *But Jesus said, "Let her alone; she has kept this for the day of My burial. For the poor you have with you always, but Me you do not have always."* (John 12:1-8)

As in the earlier passage, Mary again is focused on Jesus. As an act of worship, she anoints Him with very expensive fragrant oil worth around $25,000. Oblivious to everyone else, she had heard from the Spirit through her intimate relationship with God and obeyed in humble submission even though some close to Jesus criticized her harshly. Jesus defended her actions and exposed the misplaced judgments of her critics.

This passage also illustrates a second aspect of having a fulfilling relationship with Jesus through the actions of Lazarus. He was simply hanging out and fellowshipping with Jesus as a friend, enjoying a meal with Him and others. He didn't have to be the one preparing or serving the meal. He didn't have to hang on every word Jesus said but was free to enjoy His friendship and His company. This is what it means to fellowship with Jesus. It is not something super spiritual but it is supernaturally natural. Do we fellowship with Jesus as we enjoy a meal together with other

Christians? Do we just hang out with Him when He is in our midst as we seek to honor Him?

In this passage, Martha's actions illustrate the third aspect of a fulfilling relationship with Jesus. She is serving Him, focusing on trying to make things special for everyone. She was motivated by love and gratitude, wanting to honor Jesus.

In the earlier passage, she had a lot on her plate and was getting caught up in her "to do" list. She had lost her focus on Jesus and was losing her peace. By adjusting her priorities and scaling down on serving, she could be at peace and give her sister the freedom she needed. This earlier passage shows us the Lord does not want us to exhaust ourselves in serving Him when it takes our peace, leads us to worry, and drains our energy. Unless it is a priority ordained by God, we should be free to let some tasks go rather than continue to desperately seek help from others to "finish what needs to be done."

On the other hand, it would be a mistake to underestimate the importance of serving when it is done with a servant's heart and a loving motive. Jesus gave serving a very high priority: "And He sat down, called the twelve, and said to them, 'If anyone desires to be first, he shall be last of all and servant of all' " (Mark 9:35). He also set an example for us through washing the feet of His disciples. When the Lord directs us to serve others, we are serving Him. For example, we are to submit to our bosses and to each other as unto the Lord (see Ephesians 6:5).

The best place to be is to just flow with Jesus through the leading of the Holy Spirit. We may transition from worship to serving, to fellowship and back again, but not necessarily in any given order. We can enjoy Jesus's company and be able to relate to Him in our shared humanity. We can be reverently caught up in worshipping Him, realizing how special and unique He is as the proper object of our devotion. We can wholeheartedly serve Him with a joyful heart, letting Him know we love and appreciate Him through our words and deeds.

Jesus is inviting us to learn how to enjoy the many facets of a fulfilling and growing relationship with Him through worship, service, and fellowship. May we take Him up on it!

Chapter 2–The Goal: How to Enjoy a Fulfilling Relationship with God

Pray, Study, Meditate, and Do

Key Scripture: *"There they made Him a supper; and Martha served, but Lazarus was one of those who sat at the table with Him. Then Mary took a pound of very costly oil of spikenard, anointed the feet of Jesus, and wiped His feet with her hair. And the house was filled with the fragrance of the oil."* John 12:2-3

Ask God to help you as you work through this devotional study. Feel free to add to or change your answers at any time. You are encouraged to write all your answers.

1. During this week take some time to ask God to show you how you are doing in serving, fellowshipping with, and worshipping Him.
2. After listening to God and examining your own heart how do you think you may better serve the Lord?

3. After listening to God and examining your own heart how do you think you may better fellowship with the Lord?
4. After listening to God and examining your own heart how do you think you may better worship the Lord?
5. Consider these Bible passages. Identify and write down how the Lord is served as expressed in each passage. Matthew 10: 5-8; Matthew 14:13; Mark 10:42-45; Isaiah 6: 1-10
6. Consider these Bible passages. Identify and write down how to fellowship with the Lord is as expressed in each passage. Luke 22: 14-21; Matthew 26:36-46; John 2:1-11; Matthew 17:1-9; Luke 19:1-10
7. Consider these Bible passages. Identify and write down how the Lord is worshipped as expressed in each passage. Luke 7:36-50; Luke 5:4-8; Revelation 4:10-11; Job 42:1-8; Genesis 22:1-12
8. Use a concordance if necessary or an Internet search engine and find a few other Bible passages speak of how you can serve the Lord. Write down the references and identify how the Lord is served in each passage.
9. Use a concordance if necessary or an Internet search engine and find a few other Bible passages speak of how you can fellowship with the Lord. Write down the references and identify how you can fellowship with the Lord in each passage.
10. Use a concordance if necessary or an Internet search engine and find a few other Bible passages speak of how you can worship the Lord. Write down the references and identify how the Lord is worshipped in each passage.
11. Identify one area where you think you can work on serving the Lord better and write it down. Be specific.
12. Identify one area where you think you can work on fellowshipping with the Lord better and write it down. Be specific.
13. Identify one area where you think you can work on worshipping the Lord better and write it down. Be specific.

14. Choose one of the things God has shown you about serving, fellowshipping with, or worshipping the Lord and work on making it into a habit and incorporating it into your life. Of course, you may choose more if you wish. Input it into your mobile device or write it on a 3" by 5" index card and carry it with you. Review it several times a day. See how you do and chart your progress.

Recommended resources and/or projects for those who want to go deeper: Read Matthew 10. According to this passage, how does Jesus want His disciples to worship, serve, and fellowship with Him?

3

Where Do You Start? With a Manger in Your Heart!

Jesus replied, "Very truly I tell you, no one can see the kingdom of God unless they are born again." John 3:3 (NIV)

How do we begin to develop a proper relationship with Jesus? Let's take a look at the place and circumstances of His birth to get some insight. As we know, Jesus was born in a humble shelter, a place where animals were kept. He was wrapped in swaddling clothes to keep Him warm and comfortable. Then He was laid in a manger for comfort, safety, and security.

As you may know, a manger is a feeding trough for animals such as horses, donkeys, and cattle. But did you know, according to the research of one diligent pastor/writer, the manger where Jesus was laid was hewn out of stone? A stone manger would endure for a very long time without having to be replaced and it could be easily cleaned with water. Let's keep this in mind as we consider the human heart.

The human heart may refer to the organ in our chest that keeps the blood pumping through the body. Without its proper function, we will die physically. The heart also refers to the center of a person's life, what they truly believe, and where their inner motivations and dreams are kept. It is the place where their deepest desires are found and their most important decisions are made. Our hearts form the wellsprings of our lives but they can and do change.

In the *Parable of the Sower* (Mark 4:1-20), Jesus talks about four types of soil but he is really talking about our hearts. In a similar way, a *stony heart* can be considered as too hard to receive the Word of God so Satan snatches it away and it bears no fruit. The Old Testament references a heart of stone: "I will give you a new heart and put a new spirit in you; I will remove from you your heart of stone and give you a heart of flesh" (Ezekiel 36:26, NIV). This passage shows God's redemptive work in changing our hearts and reconnecting us to Him.

Let's now return to the manger where Jesus was born. First, there had to be room in the manger to hold Him. Then a place had to be prepared for Him. In the same way, we need to prepare a place in our hearts for Jesus to live. Even if our hearts have been like stone we can open them up for Him and let Him change us. Like the manger, our hearts can also be cleansed through the washing of water–the water of the Word of God.

From the moment we are born, we are on a spiritual pilgrimage and our hearts are engaged. When we come to realize we are far from perfect, we are on the right track. When we recognize changing our lives into what we would like them to be is more than we can do, we are moving in the right direction. When we despair of finding the resources within ourselves to overcome the inertia of remaining trapped in self-centeredness, we are at the door to a new life only God can provide.

Jesus said, "Enter by the narrow gate; for wide is the gate and broad is the way that leads to destruction, and there are many who go in by it. Because narrow is the gate and difficult is the way which leads to life, and there are few who find it." (Matthew 7:13-14). Although Jesus still speaks with authority, many people don't believe Him. They are not awakened to the true nature of reality. They also lack a sense of desperation for the need for a radical change in their lives.

Those who are desperate for answers to the pressing problems of life will persist in seeking, asking, and knocking. They may even turn to God. They are like a person who is drowning, desperately seeking air, knowing their very life depends on finding it soon. God gives them this promise: "If you seek Me with all your heart you will find Me" (see Jeremiah 29:13).

So what can we do if we have a cold and stony heart? The Good News is God is in the business of replacing cold stony hearts with warm fleshy hearts. He gives us new hearts, hearts where Jesus can live. These are hearts where real love can abide and freely flow out to others to offer them hope and healing.

When we are given a new heart, our spirits have been reborn and they are alive to God. However, we are like a helpless infant and we need help to be established in this new spiritual life with God. We need fathers, mothers, mentors, and teachers to help us to grow up through babyhood, childhood, and adolescence into maturity.

The key to maturity is in the transformation of our souls so our lives and character are a reflection of the life and character of Jesus. This important and challenging work requires a lot of grace and perseverance. It cannot be done without a humble reliance on the Spirit of God and diligently studying and meditating of the Scriptures.

The Holy Spirit is the Author of the Scriptures and the initiator of the new birth we experience when we receive Jesus into our lives and hearts. He is our primary Teacher although He uses many human teachers along the way. He knows what we need and He wants to provide it for us. He requires us to trust and yield ourselves to Him. This is how He imparts spiritual knowledge and wisdom. It comes to us as we yield control of our lives to Him. In God's economy, walking in obedience to His known will brings further revelation (John 10:27). We must ask for wisdom and believe we will receive it if we are to grow to spiritual maturity (James 1:5, Luke 2:52). So how do we enter the Kingdom of God?

We come into the Kingdom of God as an infant, a new believer in Christ. We came to realize we did not measure up to what God requires. Then we put our faith in Christ as our sin-bearer and as the One who paid the penalty for our sins. We also opened our hearts to Jesus to receive the life He provides. This is an overcoming life filled with resurrection power, the power that raised Jesus from the dead. Unfortunately, many who come to Jesus and have been born again do not go on to maturity. But what is the value of maturity?

Mature disciples can have deeper fellowship with God and He can use them in greater ways to bring many sons and daughters into the circle of His unending love. They walk by faith and don't have to understand everything before they are willing to obey God. They are trained to recognize His voice and will faithfully follow Jesus. Such people trust God and know He will enable them to do what He wants them to do. But how do we become mature?

The path to maturity requires us to cooperate with the Holy Spirit and renew our minds with the Word of God, the Holy Bible. Our thoughts and belief systems need to be changed. Our world view, the way we view reality, needs to be changed. Our thinking needs to be realigned with the truth. The truth is what God says about reality.

As we meditate on God's truths we become better able to detect thoughts and beliefs inconsistent with them and replace the lies with the truth. As our thinking and what we believe gets replaced with what is true, our souls will be transformed. We will be conformed into the image of Christ. Then we will think, believe, speak, and act in a manner consistent with His character as revealed in the Holy Bible.

God's purpose in giving us a new life is for us to share His life for all of eternity. He wants us to partake in the harmony and beauty of the life of the Father, the Son, and the Holy Spirit. As we turn our backs on all things that separate us from God and turn to Him, He will cleanse us from our sins and infuse His new life into us. Over time as we continue this process, whole tracts of our old life will be replaced by His new life. Jesus Christ will be made visible through us to a watching, skeptical, and often hostile world.

We begin our journey by receiving Jesus into our hearts through humbly opening our deepest selves to Him. It doesn't matter if we have had a cold and hard heart. What matters is we are willing to receive Him and allow Him to change us and give us a new warm heart of flesh.

Chapter 3–Where Do You Start? With a Manger in your Heart!

Pray, Study, Meditate, and Do

Key Scripture: *Jesus replied, "Very truly I tell you, no one can see the kingdom of God unless they are born again."* John 3:3 (NIV)

Ask God to help you as you work through this devotional study. Feel free to add to or change your answers at any time. You are encouraged to write all your answers.

1. What is the first prerequisite for being a disciple of Jesus Christ?
2. What are some key characteristics of a heart and life that is prepared to offer Jesus a home?
3. Is becoming a disciple mandatory for a person who has been born again? See Matthew 16:24.
4. Read Luke 14:25-33. According to this passage, what is the cost of becoming a disciple?
5. What are some benefits of becoming a disciple?
6. Read Matthew 16:24-28. What are the benefits of discipleship listed in this passage? How does this compare to your answer to Question 5?
7. Use a concordance if necessary or an Internet search engine and find some other Bible passages that address the cost of discipleship. Write down the references and identify the costs.
8. Try to find some Bible passages that identify the benefits of becoming a disciple. Write the references down and what benefits they point to.
9. Examine yourself honestly before God. What value do you place on the benefits of becoming a disciple (low, medium, high, very high, "must-have")?
10. Examine your heart before God and ask Him to show you some areas where you are struggling in deciding whether it is worthwhile to become a disciple. Write them down. Ask Him to help you surrender these areas to Him.
11. If you have resolved to follow Jesus, examine your heart before God and ask him to show you some areas where you are struggling in becoming His disciple. Write them down. Take some time this week to pray and ask Him to help you and give you

some keys that will move you forward in these areas. Write them down.

12. Choose one of the things God has shown you about becoming a disciple and work on making it into a habit and incorporating it into your life. Input it into your mobile device or write it on a 3" by 5" index card and carry it with you. Review it several times a day. See how you do and chart your progress.

Recommended resources and/or projects for those who want to go deeper: *Absolute Surrender* by Andrew Murray; *The Cost of Discipleship* by Dietrich Bonhoeffer

The Heart of the Problem Is the Problem of the Heart

Chapters 4-7

Do not be surprised if you experienced challenges along the way as you immersed yourself in the first three devotional studies. The sources of many of these challenges will be explored as you continue on this journey. You will discover the main challenge hindering you on your road to Christian maturity is the problem of the heart. The next four studies will help you understand and navigate through the challenges in your own heart that hinder you from following the Lord.

What does a lighthouse have to do with the heart of the problem being the problem of the heart? Well, a lighthouse is there for ships to find safe passage and safe harbor. Jesus is the Light of the world and we are to shine to draw others to Him. We all go through storms and rough waters. Our faith can be shipwrecked. We may not have believed in God or may have believed in false gods. None of them can help us navigate the storms of life and guide us to a safe passage home. Only the lighthouse built on the Rock. Others shone the light of Jesus for us and were used to draw us to a safe harbor in Christ. Our faith may have been shipwrecked and someone in the lighthouse spotted us, braved the rough waves, and rescued us. Now it is our turn.

4

WHO IS THE PRODIGAL?

And he said to him, "Son, you are always with me, and all that I have is yours. It was right we should make merry and be glad, for your brother was dead and is alive again, and was lost and is found." Luke 15:31-32

You probably heard the story of a young man who left his father's home to explore what the world had to offer. After indulging his senses and the desires of his heart he spent his inheritance and wound up broke in a foreign land at a time of famine. Eventually, he came to his senses and decided to return to his father and humble himself. He confessed his youthful foolishness to his father and offered to work as a hired hand, knowing he was no longer worthy to be called his son. This is perhaps the most beloved and famous story in the Bible, the parable of *The Prodigal Son*.

But how do we apply this parable? Many of us may have been blessed to be brought up in a good home where we had loving parents and a safe and secure environment with all of our needs supplied. But some of us did not have these blessings. Some of us were raised by a single parent and hardly had enough to eat. Some of us may have been raised in foster homes or in an orphanage and may not even remember our mother or father. So who might be the prodigal?

As I looked back at my own life and examined my own heart I could find the prodigal in me. At various stages of my life as a Christian, I have been led astray or drifted away from God to pursue what I believed would bring me the most fulfillment and happiness. In some ways, there is still a prodigal in me. If you review your own pilgrimage and see into your heart I believe you may also find the story of the prodigal is your story even though the details may be different. We'll examine the life of the prodigal son in the Gospel of Luke to see where we may fit in.

Luke, chapter 15 contains three parables. The first two, the *Parable of the Lost Sheep* and the *Parable of the Lost Coin*, set the context for the *Parable of the Prodigal Son*. We can read them below.

> *Then all the tax collectors and the sinners drew near to Him to hear Him. And the Pharisees and scribes complained, saying, "This Man receives sinners and eats with them." So He spoke this parable to them, saying:*

> *"What man of you, having a hundred sheep, if he loses one of them, does not leave the ninety-nine in the wilderness, and go after the one which is lost until he finds it? And when he has found it, he lays it on his shoulders, rejoicing. And when he comes home, he calls together his friends and neighbors, saying to them, 'Rejoice with me, for I have found my sheep which was lost!' I say to you likewise there will be more joy in heaven over one sinner who repents than over ninety-nine just persons who need no repentance.*

"Or what woman, having ten silver coins, if she loses one coin, does not light a lamp, sweep the house, and search carefully until she finds it? And when she has found it, she calls her friends and neighbors together, saying, 'Rejoice with me, for I have found the piece which I lost!' Likewise, I say to you, there is joy in the presence of the angels of God over one sinner who repents."

Then He said: "A certain man had two sons. And the younger of them said to his father, 'Father, give me the portion of goods that falls to me.' So he divided to them his livelihood. And not many days after, the younger son gathered all together, journeyed to a far country, and there wasted his possessions with prodigal living. But when he had spent all, there arose a severe famine in that land, and he began to be in want. Then he went and joined himself to a citizen of that country, and he sent him into his fields to feed swine. And he would gladly have filled his stomach with the pods the swine ate, and no one gave him anything.

"But when he came to himself, he said, 'How many of my father's hired servants have bread enough and to spare, and I perish with hunger! I will arise and go to my father, and will say to him, "Father, I have sinned against heaven and before you, and I am no longer worthy to be called your son. Make me like one of your hired servants."'

"And he arose and came to his father. But when he was still a great way off, his father saw him and had compassion, and ran and fell on his neck and kissed him. And the son said to him, 'Father, I have sinned against heaven and in your sight, and am no longer worthy to be called your son.'

"But the father said to his servants, 'Bring out the best robe and put it on him, and put a ring on his hand and sandals on his feet. And bring the fatted calf here and kill it, and let us eat and be merry; for this my son was dead and is alive again; he was lost and is found.' And they began to be merry.

"Now his older son was in the field. And as he came and drew near to the house, he heard music and dancing. So he called one of the servants and asked what these things meant. And he said to him, 'Your brother has come, and because he has received him safe and sound, your father has killed the fatted calf.'

"But he was angry and would not go in. Therefore his father came out and pleaded with him. So he answered and said to his father, 'Lo, these many years I have been serving you; I never transgressed your commandment at any time; and yet you never gave me a young goat, that I might make merry with my friends. But as soon as this son of yours came, who has devoured your livelihood with harlots, you killed the fatted calf for him.'

"And he said to him, 'Son, you are always with me, and all I have is yours. It was right we should make merry and be glad, for your brother was dead and is alive again, and was lost and is found.'" (Luke 15:1-32)

This passage shows we must each come to the point where we recognize we need to hear from Jesus and make the effort to draw near to Him. The tax collectors and sinners understood this but the Pharisees and scribes did not. They were self-appointed judges without compassion and didn't see their need for Jesus. Those who chose to draw near and learn from Him discovered He received them, wanted to spend time with them, and was happy to share a meal with them. Have we come to that point in our lives where we recognize our continual need to draw near and learn from Jesus? Have we drifted into being self-righteous judges, shutting out compassion toward those who are different? Are we willing to embrace those whom society looks down upon?

In these other two parables, each loss was deeply felt. Both the shepherd and the woman rearranged their schedules and priorities to search for what had been lost. The shepherd left the flock in the wilderness while he diligently searched for his lost sheep. The woman carefully searched her house to find her lost coin. Both the woman and the shepherd rejoiced when they found what they had been looking for. It was a cause for celebration! Friends and neighbors were invited to join in celebrating the good news. That which had been lost was found!

These three parables were intended to benefit everyone listening. Although they didn't know it, the Pharisees and scribes were more lost than the tax collectors and sinners who had come to Jesus and listened to what He had to say. Jesus was holding up a mirror. Would the Pharisees and scribes see themselves and repent of their hard hearts? Would they realize God is a loving Father? Would they realize He would receive them gladly with open arms if they turned to Him in faith, admitting their sin? Would they realize that He loved them even if they failed to keep His laws?

These parables also show us the condition of our own hearts. Do we realize God loves us when we fail miserably and equally loves us when we are without compassion and self-righteous judges? Do we highly value and diligently seek to bring lost people to Jesus? Are we like the shepherd who sought the lost sheep by name? Are we like the woman who diligently sought her lost coin?

We recognize the value of a dollar and understand it does not change based on its external condition. If it were wadded up, trampled through the mud, or fresh from the bank its value would be the same. Neither do we determine its value. It has an intrinsic value set by the government and market forces. But do we look at people the same way? Do we see each person of equal intrinsic value regardless of their past, present, or future condition or circumstances? Do we really believe their value is assigned by God and is unalterable? Just as the lost coin did not decrease in value to the woman and the lost sheep did not decrease in value to the shepherd, a lost person does not decrease in value to God.

We should not make the same mistake as the Pharisees and scribes by devaluing people based on external circumstances or their conduct, no matter how reprehensible it may be. This lesson was for the Pharisees and scribes and may also be for us. Have we learned it? If our compassion has been blocked through judging fellow human beings for one reason or another, we have not learned the lesson Jesus wants to teach us here.

The prodigal son in the parable took his inheritance prematurely before his father died. He valued freedom, affluence, and pleasure more than his relationship with his father. He left his father's home and presence and wandered away in search of adventure and a more satisfying life. He had wanderlust and it needed to be cured.

Before too many years had passed, he realized he was following an illusion. His dream for something more and better than what he had with his father lacked substance or a realistic hope for fulfillment. He squandered his inheritance. His desire to take his inheritance from his father and find a better life had been premature and had led him in the wrong direction. The truth is more than a few of us have been like him and prematurely took what God or our parents had to offer, left them, and squandered what they had given us.

In the parable the prodigal's disillusionment set in when he had spent his inheritance and famine overtook the land, leaving him destitute. Such disillusionment is vital and a necessary step to bring us into contact with reality. It means the deceptive illusion is coming to an end. More times than not, this experience will be very painful.

The prodigal son came to realize he would be better off returning to his father, even if he were treated as a hired hand. He also recognized he had made a series of not only bad decisions but sinful ones. He had violated God's commandments wantonly and had hurt his father. But his life had become so miserable until finally he was prepared to face the music. He thought he would come clean with his Dad and throw himself on his mercy, hoping to be treated as a hired hand. He realized he had already squandered his inheritance and his behavior had forfeited his right to be received as a son.

But the father's heart went out to his son. He knew he had to release him so he could find out for himself how empty the promises of the world could be. The father never lost hope. He looked for his son every day even though he did not know if or when he would return.

One day, he saw a figure approaching from the distance. Perhaps it was the gait or the appearance, or maybe something indefinable. But what started as an imperceptible intuition grew to an unmistakable hope in the heart of the father as his eyes locked onto the approaching figure. It was a time of great joy when the father perceived his lost son had returned home! With hope and faith welling up in his heart, he ran toward him. He saw it was indeed his son! He fell on his neck and kissed him in a profuse display of affection. Eventually, his son had an opportunity to speak and said, "Father, I have sinned against heaven and in your sight, and am no longer worthy to be called your son."

The father would have none of it! It was as if he did not hear and the son had not even spoken. His compassionate heart of love welcomed him as he extended his arms and hugged his son with a long and loving embrace. He quickly gave orders for the son to be clothed in his best robe and for him to be given one of his own signet rings, enabling him to conduct business and access wealth in the father's name. The son was given a pair of new sandals signifying he was welcomed back into the household of his father. His father then ordered the servants to prepare the fattened calf for a sumptuous feast. A great celebration was going to be given to honor the return of his lost son.

But the older brother who had loyally stayed with his father, never venturing out on his own was upset about all the love and attention his father lavished on his undeserving younger brother. He felt deprived of past opportunities to use some of his father's wealth to party with his friends. He had no intention of celebrating but was in a bitter, foul mood. Perhaps he felt his younger brother would now deprive him of his future inheritance. His father came out to plead with him to join in the celebration, explaining his brother had been lost but was now found! He had been dead but was now restored to life!

The father's explanation didn't seem to do much good. The older brother never understood his father's heart. He thought his father was strict and not fair. He thought he had to obey all the rules to receive blessings from his father but, even when he did all this, they were not forthcoming. He didn't understand all the father's wealth was his and all he had to do was ask. He didn't understand his father had the same love for him and his prodigal brother and would give anything for either of them. He didn't know both he and his younger brother were much more valuable to his father than all of his considerable wealth.

Jesus saw the Pharisees and scribes as the prodigals who had not yet returned to the Father. He was trying to help them see the true conditions of their hearts and help them understand they missed the loving Father heart of God, God wanted to withhold nothing back from them too. I can't help but believe some among the scribes and Pharisees realized this celebration and display of affection the father had for the prodigal was also intended for them. Their spirits would be moved deeply as they began to better grasp the greatness of God's love for them and for the ones they had judged.

Can you see the heart of Jesus and the heart of His Father in this parable? This is why Jesus told the story. It was to reveal the compassionate heart of God toward each one of us. Those who have faithfully and dutifully sought God without knowing His heart for them have not really understood that God will withhold no good thing from them. All they have to do is ask in faith, believing.

Those who have left the conscious presence of God looking for fulfillment outside of His will must come to an end of themselves. They must come to disillusionment in order to be brought into reality, the reality of the Father's love for them. It often takes severe circumstances to bring this about. They need to come to an end of believing they have the ability to live life on their own where God is only an option. Just as the older brother has to recognize his own self-righteousness and repent, they may need to square with God and admit they have rebelled against Him and broken His moral and righteous laws. They need to return to His love, forgiveness, and mercy. Then they can let Him decide the course of their lives. Like the prodigal son in the parable, they will be glad they did!

God will welcome those who return to Him with open arms and throw a big party in their honor. He will give them His robe of righteousness to cover all of their guild, sin, and shame. He will clothe them with honor instead. He will give them His signet ring so they have the authority of the Father backing them up. He will cover their feet with His sandals so they can walk in peace and calm troubled waters wherever they go. They had been dead but have been brought back to life. They were lost but now are found. Their return from the dead will be cause for a great celebration!

Do you, like me, see yourself in this parable and recognize you have not known the Father's heart? Perhaps you have left the Father's presence in search of a life outside of His will? Have you become disillusioned with your present life, finding it not to be what you had wanted? All you need to do is determine to come back to the Father and throw yourself on His mercy. If you do this, as one prodigal returning home to another, let me be the first to join the Father in welcoming you back home!

Chapter 4–Who Is the Prodigal?

Pray, Study, Meditate, and Do

Key Scripture: *And he said to him, "Son, you are always with me, and all that I have is yours. It was right we should make merry and be glad, for your brother was dead and is alive again, and was lost and is found."* Luke 15:31-32

Ask God to help you as you work through this devotional study. Feel free to add to or change your answers at any time. You are encouraged to write all your answers.

1. During this week take some time to examine your life and search your heart before God. Ask Him to show you whether you also

have been a prodigal. Write down your conclusion and what He showed you to justify it.
2. Can you identify a time in your life when you wanted to take what the Lord had given you and go carve out an independent life in search of greater fulfillment? Write down what you took as your "inheritance," what you were searching for, and how it worked out for you.
3. Can you identify a time in your life when you felt like the older brother faithfully doing your duty but not sensing the Father's love for you, feeling you had to work for everything you got. Write down how you felt and ask the Lord to show you what caused these feelings. Ask Him to lead you to the truth about what He thinks about you. Ask Him to lead you to scriptures that show you the truth. Write them down and meditate on them.
4. Can you identify when you, like the prodigal, had moved away from the Lord and then returned to Him? Did you sense His love and wholehearted acceptance? Describe what happened and write down how you felt after you returned to Him.
5. Consider these Bible passages. Identify and write down what they say about how God views you as expressed in each passage.

John 3:16-17 (Personalize these verses by reading them as if they were written just for you.)

Isaiah 43:1-5a

Romans 8:1-2

Hebrews 8:6-12

Ezekiel 16:1-14

Luke 22:31-32

John 21:15-19

6. Use a concordance if necessary or an Internet search engine and find some other Bible passages that show how God views you as His son. Write down the references and identify what they say about how God views you and what privileges He gives you. As you meditate on these verses, write down how they make you feel.
7. Try to find Bible passages that identify how God views us when we faithfully do our duty and don't depart from Him. Write the references down and what they reveal about the nature of God as Father. Meditate on these verses and write down how they make you feel.
8. Have you felt you have been like the older brother in the parable and you don't really relate to God as a beloved son would relate to his loving Father? Ask God to show you why you felt or still feel that way. Write down what He shows you. Meditate on the truth of how He feels about you. You can use the passages in Question 5 or find additional ones to mediate on where God speaks to you and confirms that you are a son.
9. Choose one of the truths God has shown you about how He views you and work on incorporating it into your identity before Him where it affects how you view yourself and how you live your life. Input it into your mobile device or write it on a 3" by 5" index card and carry it with you. Review it several times a day. See how you do and chart your progress.

Recommended resources and/or projects for those who want to go deeper:

Song of Songs (Song of Solomon) – Focus on how the Shulammite was viewed by Solomon and others. See the *Song of Songs* as an illustration of how the Lord views His bride and how she looks at Him, remembering we are the bride of Christ.

Prodigals and Those Who Love Them by Ruth Bell Graham

5

Fence Straddlers

"For the LORD your God is a consuming fire, a jealous God." (Deuteronomy 4:24; NIV)

Have you ever been labeled as a *fence straddler*? Would you rather be labeled as a *middle-of-the-roader*? Most of us like to avoid extremes and find common ground when we are sharing ideas or seeking solutions with our friends and associates. This is necessary and healthy, enabling us to work as a team to get things done. Most of us would prefer being known as one who is willing to compromise. But we would bristle at being called a fence straddler. So what's the difference? Let's take a closer look.

You have probably heard of *half-and-half*, the mixture of half milk and half cream, often added to coffee. Perhaps you're one of the millions who have used it to guarantee a richer taste of cream without loading the coffee up with too many calories. Similarly coffee blended 50% caffeinated and 50% decaf gives a lift without overloading on the caffeine. These strategies were seen as a happy middle ground for many coffee lovers.

We Christians in our Western culture may also seek to find a similar happy middle ground in our commitment to Christ. We want to enjoy a life of freedom and prosperity while acknowledging we are followers of Jesus. We would like to avoid making ourselves or others uncomfortable with our version of Christianity. But does biblical Christianity work this way? If you are ready to digest some spiritual meat that may choke a babe in Christ, let's forge on ahead and see what the Bible says about this.

You may recall the Church of Laodicea in the book of Revelation. This church had a lukewarm commitment to Christ. Jesus let them know how He felt about their being lukewarm and where it would lead them. This is what He said.

> *"And to the angel of the church of the Laodiceans write,*
>
> *'These things says the Amen, the Faithful and True Witness, the Beginning of the creation of God: "I know your works, you are neither cold nor hot. I could wish you were cold or hot. So then, because you are lukewarm, and neither cold nor hot, I will vomit you out of My mouth. Because you say, 'I am rich, have become wealthy, and have need of nothing'—and do not know you are wretched, miserable, poor, blind, and naked—I counsel you to buy from Me gold refined in the fire, that you may be rich; and white garments, that you may be clothed, that the shame of your nakedness may not be revealed; and anoint your eyes with eye salve, that you may see. As many as I love, I rebuke and chasten. Therefore be zealous and repent. Behold, I stand at the door and knock. If anyone hears My voice and opens the door, I will come in to him and dine with him, and he with Me. To him who overcomes I will grant to sit with Me on My throne, as I also overcame and sat down with My Father on His throne.*

> *"He who has an ear, let him hear what the Spirit says to the churches."'"* (Revelation 3: 14-22)

We must not dismiss Jesus's motivation for confronting the Laodiceans. It was because He loved them dearly. As we can see, Jesus was not too thrilled with their divided loyalty and lukewarm attitude toward Him. Why do you suppose this was so important to Him? It's all about relationships. What kind of a relationship does He want with us?

Dating relationships vary from casual to very serious. Those who date seriously want a solid commitment to show they are a high priority in the life of their friend. This does not always happen. The interests and priorities of each person often take them in different directions. Mature couples know a good marriage requires balancing other obligations and interests with their commitment and duty to their spouses. They also recognize there is no room to entertain an emotional, sexual, financial, or other bonding that compromises the marriage relationship. They understand the level of commitment in the exclusive relationship of marriage demands the needs and interests of one's spouse be given a higher priority than those in any other human relationship.

When we understand God is a jealous God and we are the bride of Christ, we can see why a divided heart, a heart not fully committed to our Lord is an offense to God and His Son. God has a right to expect us to be exclusively committed to Him at the highest level, even above the level of commitment we should have to our spouse. Have we considered the unfathomable pain Jesus endured when He paid the dowry price for His bride through pouring out His life on the cross? It was a very heavy price but the only way His bride could be purchased. He gladly gave His all for His bride because of His great love for her.

In return, God instructs and expects us to set our hearts and minds on Him and His purposes (see Colossians 3). This is totally appropriate in view of what Christ has done for us.

> *If then you were raised with Christ, seek those things which are above, where Christ is, sitting at the right hand of God. Set your mind on things above, not on things on the earth. For you died, and your life is hidden with Christ in God. When Christ who is our life appears, then you also will appear with Him in glory.*
>
> *Therefore put to death your members which are on the earth: fornication, uncleanness, passion, evil desire, and covetousness, which is idolatry. Because of these things the wrath of God is coming upon the sons of disobedience, in which you yourselves once walked when you lived in them.* (Colossians 3:1-7)

God wants us to know Him intimately and enter into the oneness of the Trinity. This is an incredible privilege and honor. We cannot plumb the depth of what God has in store for us in this relationship, but we know it must far transcend earthly marriage, the closest human relationship ordained by God. Jesus tells us what is most important as He defines eternal life in His high priestly intercessory prayer.

> *"And this is eternal life, they may know You, the only true God, and Jesus Christ whom You have sent."* (John 17: 3)
>
> *"Holy Father, keep through Your name those whom You have given Me, that they may be one as We are."* (John 17: 11b)

The need for undivided devotion to Jesus is also laid out in the cost of discipleship (Luke 14:26-33). It is necessary if we are to follow the

Lamb wherever He goes (Revelation 14:4). It is the price to pay if we are to overcome the world.

This world is at war against God. This war is waged over man's misguided desire of thinking he is better off to be autonomous than to enter into oneness with God. We must come to realize we cannot participate in the overcoming life of Jesus if we vacillate between two opinions. Joshua addresses this issue.

> *"Now therefore, fear the LORD, serve Him in sincerity and in truth, and put away the gods which your fathers served on the other side of the River and in Egypt. Serve the LORD! And if it seems evil to you to serve the LORD, choose for yourselves this day whom you will serve, whether the gods which your fathers served that were on the other side of the River, or the gods of the Amorites, in whose land you dwell. But as for me and my house, we will serve the LORD."* (Joshua 24:14-15)

The abundant life God has for us in Jesus Christ is a life fully devoted to the Father and requires loving God with all of our hearts, souls, minds, and strength. Christ in us enables us to love our neighbors as ourselves. However, it is not good to vacillate between two opinions. Before we decide to be "all in" or just walk away from being a true disciple of Jesus Christ, we need to count the cost.

Self-deception is not the best option. We may want what He has to offer but not really want Him. We may want joy, peace, prosperity, good health, and the good things of life but know we cannot obtain and keep them without help. We may be willing to make room for God while still wanting to retain control of our lives and having veto power over anything we find not to our liking.

God does not work that way. A "half-and-half" version of Christianity does not work in the real world. Yes, God may accept us into His kingdom. But to end up where He wants to take us (Christ-likeness and oneness with the Godhead), we need to come under the authority of the King. Are we willing to seek the truth and ask ourselves the hard questions? It is time to seek the Lord and find out if we are fully committed to Him. If not, let us wholeheartedly return to Him, trusting Him to change us.

Chapter 5 – Fence Straddlers

Pray, Study, Meditate, and Do

Key Scripture: *"For the LORD your God is a consuming fire, a jealous God."* (Deuteronomy 4:24; NIV)

Ask God to help you as you work through this devotional study. Feel free to add to or change your answers at any time. You are encouraged to write all your answers.

1. During this week take some time to search your heart before God and discover what temptations you have been confronted with that threaten to compromise your walk with the Lord.
2. Can you identify a time when you had to choose to do what seemed best to you for a loved one or to follow the Lord where He clearly spoke to you? Write down what happened, what choice you followed, and what the results were.
3. Can you identify a time when you had to choose whether to obey the Lord's explicit instructions or to do what seemed

expedient and made sense from a worldly point of view? Write down what the situation was, what choice you made, and what the consequences were.

4. Can you identify a time when you knew you were disobeying the Lord and there were consequences for others? How did that situation come to light and what did you learn from it? Write down what you learned from this situation.

5. Consider these Bible passages. Identify and write down what choice is being presented in each passage.

    1 Kings 18:21

    Genesis 22:1-2

    1 John 2:15-17

    Joshua 7

    2 Timothy 4:10

    1 Samuel 15:11-13

6. Use a concordance if necessary or an Internet search engine and find some other Bible passages that show choices people were confronted with where they had to decide whether to follow the Lord or not. Write down the references and identify the choices confronted them.

7. Try to find Bible passages that identify consequences when someone has not whole-heartedly followed the Lord but chose to compromise instead. Write the references down, what the compromise was, and what the results were.

8. Are you aware of any ongoing struggles where you believe you are following your own desires instead of the Lord's will for

your life? Ask the Lord to show you what is at the heart of the struggle and how to resolve it. Write it down.
9. Have you been tempted to compromise God's laws by marrying a person of the opposite sex who did not love and worship the Lord as you did? If you resisted the temptation what were the benefits? If you gave in to the temptation what were the consequences? What did you learn from this?
10. Consider King Solomon, known for his extraordinary wisdom. Read 1 Kings 11. What were the consequences of his marrying wives who followed other gods? What Scripture commands did he violated? Write them down.
11. Choose an area where God wants you to stop compromising. Ask God to help you to develop a habit of obeying Him in this area. Input it into your mobile device or write it on a 3" by 5" index card and carry it with you. Review it several times a day. See how you do and chart your progress.

Recommended resources and/or projects for those who want to go deeper: *The Absolutes* by James Robison

6

CIRCUMCISING OUR HEARTS

"For he is not a Jew who is one outwardly, nor is circumcision that which is outward in the flesh; but he is a Jew who is one inwardly; and circumcision is of the heart, in the Spirit, not in the letter; whose praise is not from men but from God." Romans 2:28-29

Sin is a God-sized problem. So is cleaning it up. No man, woman, or group of men and women can solve or reverse the problem of sin. The effects of sin are everywhere. Its tragic consequences affect us in the depth of our beings. Sin causes separation or alienation from God, from our true selves, and from each other. God's solution is to offer us a change of identity, including a new heart and a new spirit, which results in a new life. Only God can change the heart in such a fundamental way. Later on, He will create a new heaven and a new earth to complete His transformation and give us a new home.

Our hearts need an extreme makeover because we are too full of ourselves: our dreams, our goals, our wants, our needs, and our perspective on things. Jesus's heart was quite different. It was full of the concerns of His Father, God, and it was focused on doing God's will. He went about loving others and thinking of how to reach them with God's love as the Spirit directed Him.

God had made a covenant with Abraham, Isaac, Jacob, and their descendants. He required the Israelite males to be circumcised as a sign of this covenant. If they failed to get circumcised they would be cut off from God's covenant people. Male babies were required to be circumcised on the eighth day after their birth. Because God created the heavens and the earth in six days and rested on the seventh, the eighth day represents the first day of God's new creation when He gives a person a new heart.

Circumcision is a painful experience and required males to yield their means of reproduction through their most private part to God to cut away the flesh. Old Testament laws and the Sermon on the Mount reinforce the need to surrender our private sexual lives to God, including our secret thoughts, attitudes, and habits. God knows it may be painful to yield our private sexual lives to Him but He makes it a high priority. This area is crucial if we are to make progress in our lives as disciples of Jesus.

Although we are saved by grace we are not free to run our own public and private lives as we please. We are not saved by keeping God's laws. However, God is at work in transforming His children to bring them into conformity with the character of His Son. Jesus always kept God's laws. Jesus said, "Therefore anyone who sets aside one of the least of these commands and teaches others accordingly will be called least in the kingdom of heaven, but whoever practices and teaches these commands will be called great in the kingdom of heaven" (Matthew 5:9; NIV). God does not require us to clean up our private sexual lives to be saved but we must be willing to follow His lead. God wants us to trust Him and surrender this most important part of our lives to Him. "But just as he who called you is holy, so be holy in all you do; for it is written: 'Be holy, because I am holy.'" (1 Peter 1:5-16; NIV)

Although some Jewish believers insisted the Gentiles had to be circumcised to be saved, Paul strongly opposed such a belief. He said salvation is by faith alone and has nothing to do with keeping the law or a part of it. He said requiring someone to keep even a part of the law to be saved would separate them from grace. They would be putting themselves under the bondage of the law, trying to keep it, to earn their salvation. Such an attitude would cut them off from grace. Requiring Gentiles to be circumcised would be another gospel, where men's efforts at keeping the law helped them to reach God (see Galatians).

The issue of circumcision created such a big controversy in the early church that it required Paul to go to Jerusalem and meet with the other apostles to resolve it (see Acts, chapter 15). Although the Jerusalem council concluded the Gentiles did not need to be circumcised or keep the Law of Moses to be saved, it requested that they refrain from sexual immorality (see Acts 15:29).

What is circumcision really about? In Romans 2:25-29, Paul wrote about the purpose of circumcision and its spiritual application. It represents the challenge of separating the fleshly parts of our hearts from the new heart God has given us. He is working to "cut away the sinful flesh." He wants to circumcise our hearts. A circumcised heart is the true proof of a person being under the new covenant. As Paul said, "A Jew is one who is a Jew inwardly and circumcision is of the heart, in the Spirit."

In the ongoing process of circumcising the heart, God is at work cutting away "fleshly" habits and attitudes that reek of pride and "self." It is often a painful process that our flesh resists. Jesus explains this pruning process in the paragraphs below.

> *"I am the true vine, and My Father is the vinedresser. Every branch in Me that does not bear fruit He takes away; and every branch that bears fruit He prunes, that it may bear*

> *more fruit. You are already clean because of the word which I have spoken to you. Abide in Me, and I in you. As the branch cannot bear fruit of itself, unless it abides in the vine, neither can you, unless you abide in Me.*
>
> *"I am the vine, you are the branches. He who abides in Me, and I in him, bears much fruit; for without Me you can do nothing. If anyone does not abide in Me, he is cast out as a branch and is withered; and they gather them and throw them into the fire, and they are burned. If you abide in Me, and My words abide in you, you will ask what you desire, and it shall be done for you. By this My Father is glorified, that you bear much fruit; so you will be My disciples.*
>
> *"As the Father loved Me, I also have loved you; abide in My love. If you keep My commandments, you will abide in My love, just as I have kept My Father's commandments and abide in His love."* (John 15:1-10).

The pruning process is God's way of circumcising our hearts. God chooses what to prune and when to prune it. He knows how much we can bear. He treats us individually. There is no "one size fits all" in the way God disciplines us. His goal is to perfect our love and He is motivated by His love for us. He wants us to learn how to love Him supremely, love each other, and love ourselves in a balanced way. As we follow the Lord, we can be assured He will circumcise our hearts. He will prune away the bad habits or even the neutral or "good" habits to make room for the best.

His desire is for us to bear much fruit. I hope it's your desire too.

Chapter 6 – Circumcising Our Hearts

Pray, Study, Meditate, and Do

Key Scripture: *"For he is not a Jew who is one outwardly, nor is circumcision that which is outward in the flesh; but he is a Jew who is one inwardly; and circumcision is of the heart, in the Spirit, not in the letter; whose praise is not from men but from God."* Romans 2:28-29

Ask God to help you as you work through this devotional study. Feel free to add to or change your answers at any time. You are encouraged to write all your answers.

1. What do you think it means to circumcise the heart?
2. During this week take some time to search your heart before God and ask Him to show you some things of your fleshly nature that should be separated from your heart.
3. Why do you think the heart and the spirit are so closely linked together?
4. If circumcision was given for a sign what reality did it point to?
5. Why do you think only Jews were required to be circumcised?
6. Consider these Bible passages. Identify and write down how circumcision was used in each passage.

Acts 15: 1-24,

Exodus 4:24-26

Deuteronomy 10:16

Jeremiah 4:4

Genesis 17:1-14

John 7:22-23

7. Use a concordance if necessary or an Internet search engine and find some other Bible passages that speak of circumcision and the covenant it represents. Write down the references and identify how circumcision was used in each passage.
8. Try to find Bible passages that identify the circumcision of the heart. Write the references down and what you think the passages mean by "circumcision of the heart."
9. How do you think your heart has been circumcised in the past?
10. Can you identify some things God wants to cut away from your heart and remove from your life now? What are they?
11. How do you think God can motivate someone to be willing to participate in the painful circumcision of the heart which requires cutting away things that hurt our relationship with God? What did He do to motivate you to go through this painful process in the past?
12. Choose one of the things God has shown you that He wants to cut out of your life and seek the Lord's help to remove it. Work on making the removal of this negative influence into a habit and incorporating it into your life. Input it into your mobile device or write it on a 3" by 5" index card and carry it with you. Review it several times a day. See how you do and chart your progress.

Recommended resources and/or projects for those who want to go deeper: *Rebel with a Cause* by Franklin Graham

7

LET GOD BE YOUR HEART SURGEON

"The Lord your God will circumcise your hearts and the hearts of your descendants, so that you may love Him with all your heart and with all your soul, and live."
(Deuteronomy 30:6; NIV)

Have you ever wondered how it would be possible to obey the Greatest Commandment — to love the Lord our God with all of our hearts, souls, minds, and strength? Have you come to the realization you cannot get there on your own strength or through your own resources? Perhaps, like me, you realize this must be a work of God. But this is where I want to go. How about you?

In the Lord's providence as I sought to research where the children of Israel were blessed, I was led to Deuteronomy 30:6 (NIV): "The Lord your God will circumcise your hearts and the hearts of your descendants, so that you may love Him with all your heart and with all your soul, and live." Let's look at the longer passage in Deuteronomy 30:1-10 to add some context.

> "Now it shall come to pass, when all these things come upon you, the blessing and the curse which I have set before you, and you call them to mind among all the nations where the LORD your God drives you, and you return to the LORD your God and obey His voice, according to all I command you today, you and your children, with all your heart and with all your soul, the LORD your God will bring you back from captivity, and have compassion on you, and gather you again from all the nations where the LORD your God has scattered you. If any of you are driven out to the farthest parts under heaven, from there the LORD your God will gather you, and from there He will bring you. Then the LORD your God will bring you to the land which your fathers possessed, and you shall possess it. He will prosper you and multiply you more than your fathers. And the LORD your God will circumcise your heart and the heart of your descendants, to love the LORD your God with all your heart and with all your soul that you may live.
>
> "Also the LORD your God will put all these curses on your enemies and on those who hate you, who persecuted you. And you will again obey the voice of the LORD and do all His commandments which I command you today. The LORD your God will make you abound in all the work of your hand, in the fruit of your body, in the increase of your livestock, and in the produce of your land for good. For the LORD will again rejoice over you for good as He rejoiced over your fathers, if you obey the voice of the LORD your God, to keep His commandments and His statutes which are written in this Book of the Law, and if you turn to the LORD your God with all your heart and with all your soul."

This is good news! God will circumcise our hearts; cutting away the sinful flesh – those habits and attitudes that keep us from God and His perfect will for us. We do not have to do it! Remember the covenant of circumcision in the Old Testament where baby boys were circumcised on the eighth day (see Genesis 17:12; Luke 2:21)? You will recall God created the heavens and the earth in six days and rested on the seventh day. Fast forward to the eighth day, the day after the Sabbath, when God raised Jesus from the dead. The Scriptures teach we have been raised up with Jesus as new creations. This is why the eighth day is sometimes referred to as the first day of the new creation.

After wandering in the desert for forty years—just before entering the Promised Land—all Israelite males born in the wilderness were circumcised (see Joshua, chapter 5). They had seen the consequences of disobedience and the faithfulness of God's provision and had been trained to recognize and obey the voice of God. Their faith had grown strong and they were now ready to enter the Promised Land, conquer their enemies, and see the promises of God fulfilled. How about us? Have we wandered in the wilderness long enough to recognize God's voice and obey Him? Are we ready to walk by faith and see the fulfillment of what God has promised us?

Going back to the covenant of circumcision, the Lord established it as an outward sign that the Israelites were participants in God's covenant with Abraham. All Israelite males were required to be circumcised or they would be cut off and excluded from the covenant. God would do His part and circumcise their hearts but men had to do their parts too with the circumcision of their bodies. (See Exodus 4:24-26 where the Lord was going to kill Moses for not circumcising his son.)

Scripture teaches the circumcision that matters most is the circumcision of the heart. This is seen in both the Old and New Testaments. Physical circumcision has no value in producing salvation although the Jews still practice it. New Testament Gentile believers were not required to be circumcised or keep the Law of Moses. Jew and Gentile were brought together as one under the new covenant by putting their faith in Jesus Christ and in His finished work on the cross (Ephesians 2:15). God placed salvation in them but they had the responsibility of working it out (Philippians 2:12). God requires each of us to renew our minds with the Word of God to transform our souls (Romans 12:2).

God knows us through and through. He knows how to move us from glory to glory. He knows all about us and is sensitive to our idiosyncrasies and the minute details of our lives. No two of us are alike and God alone is fully aware of the uniqueness we each possess. If we humbly yield to Him, He will circumcise our hearts. He will remove idols and cut away unprofitable works of the flesh – desires, beliefs, thoughts, and habits – that are not part of His new creation in us.

What a relief that God Himself is in charge of the circumcision of our hearts! He will finish the task He started with each of us. He will perform the many needed surgeries and will anesthetize us for each one. He knows we are not capable of cutting away the flesh of our own hearts and it would be a disaster for us to try it on our own. He has also removed from us the responsibility of judging others concerning the state of their hearts. These are God-sized jobs and only He can do them.

We are destined to be conformed to a glorious future, the image of Jesus Christ appearing in each of us (1 John 3:2)! To God be the glory!

Chapter 7 – Let God Be Your Heart Surgeon

Pray, Study, Meditate, and Do

Key Scripture: *"The Lord your God will circumcise your hearts and the hearts of your descendants, so that you may love Him with all your heart and with all your soul, and live."* (Deuteronomy 30:6; NIV)

Ask God to help you as you work through this devotional study. Feel free to add to or change your answers at any time. You are encouraged to write all your answers.

1. During this week take some time to search your heart before God and discover where surgery may be necessary. Write down your observations.
2. Can you identify a time in your own life when you attempted to circumcise your own heart by trying to cut out a habit you thought was displeasing to God without relying on Him? How did it work out?
3. Can you identify a time when the Lord put His finger on something in your life He wanted to change and you worked with Him, trusting Him to bring about the change? How did it work out for you?
4. Can you identify a time when you wanted someone close to you to change a bad habit and you tried to make it happen? How did it work out?
5. Can you remember a time when the Lord showed you something in someone else He wanted to change and all He wanted you to do was to intercede for them? How did it work out?

6. Consider these Bible passages. Identify and write down how circumcision was an issue and what the resolution was as expressed in each passage.

    Romans 2:25-29

    Acts 11:1-18

7. Consider the Bible passages below where rash vows were made in an attempt to honor or please God. What were the consequences of those vows? What can we learn about the hearts of those making the vows, about those who were affected by the vows, and about how the conflict was resolved?

    1 Samuel 14:24-46

    Judges 11:29-39

8. Use a concordance if necessary or an Internet search engine and find some other Bible passages that show God's part in circumcising the heart. Write down the references and identify God's part according to the passages.
9. Ask God to help you find two or three Bible passages that show what happens when people try to clean up their own hearts. Write the references down, what the "heart problem" was, and what the results were when they tried to fix their heart issues without relying on God.
10. Ask God to help you find two or three Bible passages that show what happens when people try to clean up other peoples' hearts. Write down the references, the "heart problems," the attempted "fixes," and what the results were when they tried to implement the "fixes."

11. Ask God to show you an area of your heart He wants to change. Look for Him to show you what you can do to cooperate with Him as He "circumcises" your heart.
12. Ask God to show you an area of the heart of someone close to you that He wants to change. Look for Him to show you what you can do to cooperate with Him as He "circumcises" their heart. Write these things down.
13. Think about an area in the heart of someone close to you that you would like to see changed. Ask God whether what you see in them is an indication of an area of your heart that needs to be changed. Ask Him to help you to make the changes He wants you to make. Ask Him to show you how to intercede for the other person and cooperate with God so He can change the other person as He wishes.
14. Choose one of the things God has shown you where He wants to "circumcise" your heart and cooperate with Him in habitually changing that area of your heart and incorporating it into your life. Input it into your mobile device or write it on a 3" by 5" index card and carry it with you. Review it several times a day. See how you do and chart your progress.

Recommended resources and/or projects for those who want to go deeper: See if you can find some people among your close friends and family who are willing to share what happened when they tried to make fundamental changes in the lives of other people close to them; when they tried to change themselves without God's help; or when they cooperated with God in His plan to change their hearts at a fundamental level. Interview them. Write down what you learned.

Overcoming Our Worldly Culture

Chapters 8-12

How are you doing with implementing the character changes you have identified from the first seven devotional studies? Have any of them been easy? Remember inspiration is important but transformation requires discipline and determination to be successful. You will discover that hindrances to Christian maturity are both internal and external. Many come from our modern culture. We will take a look at how our worldly culture opposes Christ and how we can overcome these hindrances in the next five chapters.

We cannot be like the Loan Ranger if we are going to navigate safely through the rapids and currents in our culture that can take us far away from God and destroy our souls. Jesus provides the Boat but we all have a job to do. If we work together and pay attention to the Head (Jesus), we will make it safely through. We may even enjoy the challenge and grow in our appreciation of each other along the way!

8

LIVING IN A MORAL FREE-FALL

But know this, that in the last days perilous times will come: For men will be lovers of themselves, lovers of money, boasters, proud, blasphemers, disobedient to parents, unthankful, unholy, unloving, unforgiving, slanderers, without self-control, brutal, despisers of good, traitors, headstrong, haughty, lovers of pleasure rather than lovers of God, having a form of godliness but denying its power. And from such people turn away! 2 Timothy 3:1-5

Since the time Jesus walked the earth, we have been in what the Bible calls *the last days*. Signs of the times indicate we may be living towards the end of the last days. Jesus Christ could very well return to earth before some of us die. But, since the time of the Apostles, there have always been Christians who believed the Lord would return in their lifetime.

We should strive to be like the men of Issachar "who understood the times and knew what Israel should do" (see 1 Chronicles 12:32; NIV). The Lord wants us to be prepared for what the Bible says will happen. In

Matthew 24:12 we are warned, "Because of the increase of wickedness, the love of most will grow cold." At the end of this season of testing and trials (the last days), many believe we will go through what has been called *The Great Tribulation* right before Jesus returns. If it is our privilege to go through these great trials that severely test our faith, will we be able to answer "Yes!" to Jesus's question: "Will the Son of Man find faith on the earth when He returns?" (Luke 18:8)

Those with spiritual and moral discernment recognize we are living in *a moral free-fall* where standards of right and wrong are continually being challenged and abandoned. Biblical morality is no longer the norm in our culture. The younger generations do not share the same value system as the older generations. Accepted values of our society have continued to move toward deeper levels of immorality and depravity. The entertainment industry and mass media have flooded our minds, ears, and eyes with increasing levels of perversion and graphic violence. This flood of moral filth has desensitized us to our humanity. An increasingly large percentage of our population no longer responds to violations of basic human rights as previous generations did. We as a culture have become anesthetized to the evil around us to the point where we tune it out and it doesn't even bother us.

This moral free-fall permeates our institutions and culture. I will list a few examples here.

> A few years back the U.S. Supreme Court ruled that homosexual marriage was a Constitutional right. Those who discriminate against it can be sentenced to jail and lose their jobs, businesses, wealth, and/or reputations.

> Gender distinctions have now been blurred to the point that almost anything is considered *normal*. For instance, public bathrooms can

be used based on the gender identity preference of the user in some jurisdictions.

A recent U.S. President bypassed Congress and the Constitution by creating and appointing unelected czars, unaccountable to Congress and the people, to oversee much of the Federal government apparatus.

One major political party continually tries to undermine the legitimacy of a duly elected President through one trumped-up charge after another, with some members even supporting impeachment before he was even sworn into office.

Terrorist organizations such as ISIS have used the most callous and depraved ways of destroying those who oppose them and their goals.

Leaders of a major tax-supported organization were documented as having sold body parts of fetuses that were being harvested. The leaders were not given jail time but the undercover journalists and investigators who exposed this wickedness were subjected to lawsuits and fines and, if convicted, could serve up to ten years in jail.

The list goes on and it's a long one. How are we supposed to respond as Christians to these "signs of the times"? If we understand what God is doing and why He is allowing these things, we will be in a better position to know how to respond.

Several years ago, in the early morning hours, I heard the Lord speak three words to my heart as I was spending time seeking Him. These words were *"shake, sift, and shift."* I wondered what the Lord meant by them. The answer was not meant to be hidden. I've heard messages and Bible teachings (Hebrews 12:25-29) on *shaking* and had also heard messages on *shifting*. As I considered *sift*, the main thought that came to mind was the warning Jesus gave Peter that Satan desired to sift him like wheat. How can we successfully navigate through the present moral free-fall and remain faithful to our callings and God's purposes for our lives? I believe understanding these three words and how to apply them to our lives will help.

The Holy Bible teaches what cannot be shaken or changed include God, His Character, and His Word. For instance, Jesus said, "Heaven and earth shall pass away, but my words shall not pass away" (Matthew 24:35; KJV). In Hebrews, chapter 12, the Bible talks about the Lord shaking everything can be shaken so those things which cannot be shaken will become more apparent. In short, God determines what can and cannot be shaken.

To gain further insight let us consider the words of the Apostle Peter from 2 Peter 3:10-13.

> *But the day of the Lord will come as a thief in the night, in which the heavens will pass away with a great noise, and the elements will melt with fervent heat; both the earth and the works that are in it will be burned up. Therefore, since all these things will be dissolved, what manner of persons ought you to be in holy conduct and godliness, looking for and hastening the coming of the day of God, because of which the heavens will be dissolved, being on fire, and the elements will melt with fervent heat? Nevertheless we, according to His promise, look for new heavens and a new earth in which righteousness dwells.*

God already knows all things including the deep secrets of our hearts but He uses the shaking to sift us and to reveal to us what's in our hearts and what we truly believe. Jesus warned Peter he would be sifted. Yet Peter had more confidence in himself than he had in Jesus and contradicted Him, telling Jesus he would never forsake Him. Events unfolded just as the Lord had said and Peter went through a time of sifting. In the midst of this very painful process, Peter wept bitterly at his unfaithfulness for denying the Lord.

Jesus had warned Peter of what was to come but did not leave him without hope. Jesus encouraged Peter and promised He would pray for Peter so that his faith would not completely fail. He also prophesied to Peter that he would be restored and that he was to then strengthen his brethren. Later, Peter met Jesus after He was resurrected. Jesus asked Peter whether he loved Him more than the other disciples did. Peter affirmed his love for the Lord but, when pressed, he revealed that he had learned a valuable lesson. He acknowledged the Lord knew all things including how much Peter loved Him. Peter implicitly recognized his own limitations.

The good news for Peter was that, after the shaking and the painful time of sifting, he would be prepared to be shifted into a higher level of influence and authority to fulfill his destiny. He would continue to be used by the Lord to build God's kingdom and would eventually die a martyr's death. May we, like Peter, fulfill our destinies after our time of sifting.

I have often shared these three words (shake, sift, and shift) because I sensed they were not only personal words for me but were also for the Body of Christ in general. Since I was given these words, I have been going through a very painful time of sifting. This sifting process has revealed the true condition of my heart and character. All of my own righteousness has been revealed as tainted by my own self-interests – *filthy rags* in the eyes of the Lord. My level of maturity has been shown to be several notches below where I thought it was. Yet I have been a Christian for over forty-five years. No matter. May God accomplish what He wants with me, both in and through my life. *Not my will, but Thy will be done.* I hope you can join me in that declaration.

I believe shaking, sifting, and shifting are to be expected. Understanding this will help prepare us for God's purposes in these last days. As God continues to cause or allow this shaking, the foundations of many lives will be revealed and all that man has built apart from God will continue to crumble. Satan will also sift us during these times of shaking. But it will be under the Lord's watchful eye and He will continue to intercede for us.

When the refinement process is sufficiently complete God will shift us into the positions where we can be most effective for Him. He will provide us with the grace and power we need to further His kingdom and accomplish His will for our lives. I believe this is what the Dry Bones prophecy in Ezekiel is all about. The dry bones (God's people who had lost all hope) are being moved into place and brought back to life as they respond to God's prophetic Word. Once they are shifted into position, they will become the mighty army of God, ready to march and fight at His command. Then He will release His power through them.

We need to be prepared to go through these fiery trials and accept God's refinement process. The only way we will be able to stand against the moral free-fall is for us to be rooted and grounded in Christ. God will continue to use the shaking process to reveal our life foundation. We must have our lives carefully built on the foundation of the apostles and prophets with Jesus Christ as our Chief Cornerstone. If this is so, God's Word will abide in our hearts and be reflected through what we believe and meditate on. What we think, say, and do will line up with God's Word.

Let us not grow weary and discouraged or lose hope when we go through our fiery trials. Let us believe God and, by faith, count it all joy and not think it strange when we encounter the trials. Let us remember God's purpose is to test and refine our faith just like Simon Peter's faith was tested and refined. Let us also remember when Nebuchadnezzar, the king of ancient Babylon threw Shadrach, Meshach, and Abed-Nego into a fiery furnace (see Daniel, chapter 3), there was a fourth man like the Son of God who was in the fire with them. Even though the furnace was heated seven times hotter than normal and consumed the soldiers who threw them into the fire, God's servants came out unscathed without even the smell of smoke or a singed hair. As a result, God changed the king's heart toward them and their God. Then God was honored throughout the land because of the faithfulness of these three men through the fiery trials they were called to endure.

God will do the same for us and stand with us to preserve us in and through our fiery trials. May we also be found faithful as we rely on and encounter the Fourth Man Who stands with us in our trials–the Son of God, our Lord Jesus Christ. Then He will receive great glory as many come to Him through our purified faith which has been proven genuine.

Chapter 8 – Living in a Moral Free-fall

Pray, Study, Meditate, and Do

Key Scripture: *But know this, that in the last days perilous times will come: For men will be lovers of themselves, lovers of money, boasters, proud, blasphemers, disobedient to parents, unthankful, unholy, unloving, unforgiving, slanderers, without self-control, brutal, despisers of good, traitors, headstrong, haughty, lovers of pleasure rather than lovers of God, having a form of godliness but denying its power. And from such people turn away!* 2 Timothy 3:1-5

Ask God to help you as you work through this devotional study. Feel free to add to or change your answers at any time. You are encouraged to write all your answers.

1. During this week take some time to reflect on where our culture has departed from Biblical morality in significant ways and ask the Lord to show you how this has affected your own moral values.
2. Can you identify three "tools" that have been used to accelerate the moral free-fall of our culture? (businesses, industries, technology, etc. – be specific)
3. Can you identify three things God has given you to protect you from experiencing adverse consequences in your morality while living in an increasingly decadent culture?
4. Can you identify where your moral values have deteriorated as a result of a decline in the moral value of the culture around us?
5. Ask the Lord to show you how to recalibrate your morality to fit His standard in the Holy Bible. What ideas did He give you to help you do this?
6. Consider these Bible passages. Identify and write down indications of a breakdown in public morality as expressed in each passage.

    2 Timothy 4:2-4

    2 Timothy 3:10-17

    Judges 17

    Judges 21

    Revelation 3:14-22

7. Use a concordance if necessary or an Internet search engine and find some other Bible passages that show a major decline in the private and public morality of a culture. Write down the references and identify what particular moral problems they identify.
8. Find some Bible passages that identify how you can protect yourself from the immorality of the culture in which we live. Write the references down and what advice or commands they give to protect you from moral deterioration.
9. What have you done that has helped you resist the immorality in your culture? Be specific about what you have done and how it has helped you.
10. To see where our culture has declined morally, track changes in our laws, our educational system, and in our mass media that have paved the way.
11. God calls Christians to be "salt and light" which means to light the way for others and to help preserve what is good by our influence. Ask God to show you how you can get involved in using your gifts and your Christian witness to be "salt and light" in your world. It may be through your family, your community, your church, your business, politics, education, media, or other centers of influence. If you have already been involved in this way, thank the Lord for how He has used you and continue to follow Him in your endeavors.
12. Choose one of the things God has shown you where He wants to work with you to strengthen your moral resolve. Ask Him how and work on making it into a habit and incorporating it into your life. Input it into your mobile device or write it on a 3" by 5" index card and carry it with you. See how you do and chart your progress.

Recommended resources and/or projects for those who want to go deeper: *How Should We then Live?* by Francis Schaeffer, *Whatever Happened to the Human Race?* by Francis Schaeffer

9

BUBBLE REALITIES

In the beginning God created the heavens and the earth. ... And God said ... and it was so. (Genesis 1:1a; 7, 9, 11, 15, 24, 30; KJV)

There was the *dot com* bubble. We know how that ended. Then there was the real estate bubble and we know how that ended. There were also several stock market bubbles. They also ended poorly for many people. Bubbles eventually burst and create problems for those who put their confidence in them, believing they are an accurate assessment of reality.

Many people are living in their own "bubble" and they think it is reality. They do not recognize they are in a bubble. They are in for a hard crash unless they wake up to the fact that they are not seeing the world as it really is. Reality is designed to break through even the deepest deception. For some, it will be too late to make positive adjustments to reality but for others, their disillusionment will be in time to make a "midcourse correction" for the direction of their lives.

Why do people choose to live in the deception of a bubble reality? The main reason is they do not have a love for the truth. Those who love God and His Word will not get caught up in the delusions of bubble realities. The Holy Bible is the best book to study to get an accurate assessment of the most important realities.

A major propagator of bubble realities is the mass media, particularly the programming most Americans watch on TV, sometimes for eight or more hours a day. We have been inundated with godless programming flooding our minds and hearts with violence, sexual images and scenes, horror, the occult, and other disgusting words and images. This programming has the effect of desensitizing us to many forms of evil. For example, watching too many programs that include excessive violence makes us more passive and less inclined or able to react or respond appropriately when observing violence in the real world.

Watching too much TV can have a significant impact on skewing our sense of reality. This is especially true for young children. Have you ever watched a baby or a young child as they watch TV? I am told they do not have a good sense of distinguishing reality from the images on TV. Although research has shown the effects of TV watching on the brain, these results are not well known and have been almost completely suppressed by today's mass media outlets. Watching too much TV changes our brains, causing us to bypass critical functions, so we unknowingly and gradually accept many of the underlying values portrayed on TV. This fact alone explains why younger generations have significantly drifted from the Bible's moral code and values.

So-called TV "news" is perhaps the biggest offender in creating a bubble reality. It sets our priorities on what is newsworthy and censors or inaccurately reports much of what is truly newsworthy. As a result, most of us are not even aware of what is happening in the world around us. Those who think the government can continually provide for their needs while going deeper and deeper in debt are also living in a "bubble reality." Their lives seem to function reasonably well for a while but, sooner or later, the federal government will fail as it sinks under the weight of excessive debt.

Those who focus on the good and ignore the bad are living in a bubble reality. So are those who ignore the good and focus on the bad. Our world shows evidence of a glorious creation. We also see evidence of a tragically flawed world. True reality has a place for both. In order to adjust to true reality, we must take into account both the good and the bad in our world.

God gives us the Holy Bible as our reference point to define reality. Through it and through God's Holy Spirit of Truth we can discern the difference between what is true and what is false. Any perception of reality that does not have God as the center is a bubble reality of some sort or another. God is the definer of reality and He is sovereign. When we attune our minds to His truth, we can embrace Him and learn to live successfully in His eyes even when significant pain invades our private worlds.

It is good to recognize it is possible to live in several bubble realities at a time. Am I living in a bubble reality? Are you living in a bubble reality? What are our bubble realities? How did we enter them and what must we do to successfully exit them? These questions need to be asked and the correct answers need to be discerned. Knowing the answers will help us adjust to living in the reality that God created so we can have stability in the midst of upheavals in the world around us. We must build our lives on the truth, the Rock of Jesus Christ, not on the deceptive sand of bubble realities.

Chapter 9 – Bubble Realities

Pray, Study, Meditate, and Do

Key Scripture: *In the beginning God created the heavens and the earth. ... And God said ... and it was so.* (Genesis 1:1a; 7, 9, 11, 15, 24, 30; KJV)

Ask God to help you as you work through this devotional study. Feel free to add to or change your answers at any time. You are encouraged to write all your answers.

1. During this week take some time to search your heart before God and ask Him to show you any area of your life where you may be living in a bubble reality.
2. Can you identify three widespread bubble realities in our culture?
3. Can you identify three widespread bubble realities in other cultures?
4. What do all bubble realities have in common?
5. Consider these Bible passages. Identify and write down the bubble reality expressed in each passage.

    Genesis 6

    Genesis 11:1-9

    1 Samuel 8

    Revelation 3:14-22

Luke 17:20-37

6. Use a concordance if necessary or an Internet search engine and find some other Bible passages that show bubble realities. Write down the references and identify what bubble realities they identify.
7. Ask God to guide you and search for a few Bible passages that identify telltale signs of a culture based on a bubble reality. Write the references down and what the passages say are signs of a bubble reality.
8. Ask God to guide you and search for a few Bible passages identifying how to approach a person who is living in a bubble reality. Write the references down and the method each passage uses to approach a person living in a bubble reality.
9. How would you approach a person living in a bubble reality?
10. Ask God to show you someone or several people living in bubble realities and ask Him to show you how to pray for them. Be willing for Him to use you to approach them to help them out of their deception to a place where they can embrace the truth. Jesus Christ is the true reality.
11. If God has shown you that you are living in a bubble reality, seek the Lord and His plan to be permanently delivered out of it. Input it into your mobile device or write it on a 3" by 5" index card and carry it with you. Review it several times a day. See how you do and chart your progress.

Recommended resources and/or projects for those who want to go deeper: Identify some bubble realities in your culture and write an essay (about three pages would be good) explaining what they are, why they are bubble realities, and what you can do to help deliver those in your area of influence out of them.

10

Overcoming Distractions and Goal Setting

"For the Lord GOD will help Me; therefore I will not be disgraced; Therefore I have set My face like a flint, and I know that I will not be ashamed." Isaiah 50:7

Distractions–we all have them. I have found myself distracted from my goal of becoming a writer/author. I was advised writers need to see themselves as writers and develop a mindset where they work on writing something virtually every day. My plan was to write six days a week, spending an hour or two per day writing. But things got in the way. I got distracted.

I took up a hobby I had set aside about thirty years ago. I began playing chess again. I found chess to be a wonderful and challenging game but it could also be addicting. I decided to reach out to the younger generation. I was hoping to help them discover the joys of chess and the camaraderie it had afforded me. So I started a local chess club that also welcomed adults.

I had another reason to return to my old hobby: I didn't want a lazy brain or memory. Mine seemed to be atrophying from lack of use and watching too much TV. Chess motivated me to exercise my judgment, imagination, reasoning, logic, and memory. Taking up chess again was a good thing for me but I couldn't let it crowd out the more important strategic goal of becoming a writer. But my chess club wasn't a problem because it met only once a week for three hours at the local library.

While seeking to grow my local chess club, I discovered playing chess on the Internet. I could play timed games any time against people of similar ratings. I thought it was a golden opportunity for evangelism. Internet chess was very convenient and became a welcome break from TV and its associated snacking. It also helped me keep my weight down as I didn't snack when I played. But playing chess on the Internet became a distraction for me that began to border on addiction.

I would play chess an hour or two a day against random opponents who lived from all over the world. I would also observe the games of other players and tune in to tournaments where the best players in the world were competing. Most of my games were over in twenty to forty-five minutes. However, sometimes I spent several hours watching tournament games that could last much longer. I enjoyed the camaraderie of contributing to on-line commenting, analyzing, and light-hearted bantering during these times. But it drained me of time and energy for more productive and fruitful endeavors.

Distractions and addictions are a very serious problem in today's culture. Computer and smart-phone games can consume a lot of time as can watching TV. We program our minds and they program us. Those who market these games have their own ideas and don't mind if we get addicted. They even have a vested interest in our addiction and create games that are addicting. These addicting games are like a new kind of drug. And they are proliferating our society. So how do we deal with distractions that may become addictions?

Those who are in painful circumstances and those without a deep sense of purpose are probably most vulnerable to distractions and addictions. If you enjoy a certain activity and can do it, you often will. But do we need to limit our sources of pleasure? Taking the long view, when our lives are over, what kind of legacy will we leave? Playing chess may help my mental health and increase my sense of well being. But is there any lasting benefit if I play excessively to gain rating points and move up in standing as a chess player? How does that further God's purposes and help Him build His kingdom? I encourage you to ask similar questions if you are fighting distractions or addictions.

God's Word shows that almost everything on this earth will pass away. Only people and the Word of God will last forever. Although people die, the Bible teaches a day of resurrection is coming, both for the just and for the unjust. Jesus came to seek and to save that which was lost and He gave us the Great Commission – to go into the world and make disciples of all nations, teaching them to observe the commandments originally given to the apostles and disciples. In light of these things, how do we deal with distractions?

To live strategically we must prioritize our goals and have a workable plan that puts our top priorities first. We also need to make sure we keep our focus on our top priorities in order to accomplish them. In an interesting study, newly-graduated MBAs from Harvard Business School were asked this question: ***Have you set written goals and created a plan for their attainment?*** The graduates were tracked over time to see how successful they had become.

Those who achieved phenomenal success had a written set of goals and plans to achieve them. They also broke down their long-term goals and plans into shorter-term goals and plans. They continued to break them down until they were left with daily goals. Those who hadn't written down their goals were the least successful in reaching them. Those who had written goals without a written plan were much more successful than those with no written goals but significantly less successful than those who also had written plans to achieve their goals. Although widely circulated on the Internet there is some doubt that this study actually happened so I challenge you to write down your goals and create a plan for their attainment. In ten years, I would like to hear from you!

Experts have said it is best to write down three to five things to focus on accomplishing each day. Then check them off as you accomplish them. These experts discourage getting overly ambitious and writing down too many daily goals. If you assign yourself too many tasks you will wind up frustrating yourself when you consistently do not accomplish them all. This will be a negative motivator and discourage you.

Looking at your set of daily goals several times during the day helps you keep focused on them. Learn how to block out an appropriate time and place for you to work on your high-priority goals without distractions, especially if you don't tolerate distractions well. This might require adjusting your schedule and waking up earlier or going to bed later so you have some uninterrupted time to work on important goals. Some goals can be accomplished in the midst of mild, moderate, or even severe interruptions without sacrificing quality. You are wise to keep these things in mind as you make your schedule.

Setting realistic expectations is also important. Pursuing unrealistic expectations usually ends in frustration and negatively affects one's motivation. How many people have made New Year's resolutions only to give up on them within a month? Achievable goals are the key. You can raise the bar to include more challenging goals as you build a track record of success. You will build on your previous success so that more difficult goals will now be within your range of potential achievement. Even if you fail to reach some goals but learn from your mistakes, you will be better able to succeed in the future.

As an old Chinese proverb says, "The longest journey begins with the first step." Perfectionists may never take the first step because they are constantly modifying their plans to make them "more perfect." When they feel doomed to failure because they have set too high of a standard, they will not even try. As someone has said, "Aim for the stars. If you don't reach them, you may at least land on the moon."

Successful people know what they want and why they want it. They keep their motivation strong, make realistic plans, and monitor their progress to keep them on track. They also know how to find the help they need to achieve their goals. This is where mentors may come in. Mentors may be willing to share special knowledge and expertise to help you reach your goals. Since we were made in God's image and likeness we should look to Him to guide us in our goal setting.

God personally wrote the Ten Commandments on stone tablets. The Holy Spirit used men to write down the most important things in the Holy Bible. In Jesus's last words before He ascended into heaven, He gave His followers the Great Commission which was subsequently written down. Jesus commissioned the apostles to make disciples and commissioned them to make more disciples. A fully trained disciple is like his Master and is able to make disciples even as his Master has done. May I encourage you to write down your goals and plans? May I also encourage you to write as you answer the questions in this book and track your progress in making new godly habits with God's help?

We can help others follow Jesus to the degree that we are following Him. If He has taught us some things and shown us how to overcome in some areas we can pass that knowledge on to others to help them overcome similar challenges. "Blessed be the God and Father of our Lord Jesus Christ, the Father of mercies and God of all comfort, who comforts us in all our tribulation, that we may be able to comfort those who are in any trouble, with the comfort with which we ourselves are comforted by God." (2 Corinthians 1:3-4)

Christianity is not about "self-help." It is about yielding to the Holy Spirit and about renewing our minds with the Word of God, the Holy Bible. As our thoughts and attitudes are changed, our words and actions follow. We become transformed by the Word and the Spirit so our characters and lives follow the example of Jesus Christ. We become enabled to better love ourselves and our neighbors as ourselves. We also move closer to loving the Lord our God with all that is within us – heart, soul, mind, and strength.

Satan uses distractions to get us off the path God has for us. God wants us to love and to make disciples. This requires discipline and perseverance. It requires knowing and applying the Scriptures to our situations and challenges. It requires yielding to the Holy Spirit and living a disciplined life. You will note the two words "disciple" and "discipline" look similar and are closely related. A disciple must have discipline. In order for us to fulfill our God-given destiny, we will have to learn how to effectively deal with distractions. This will require living a disciplined life.

Chapter 10 – Overcoming Distractions and Goal Setting

Pray, Study, Meditate, and Do

Key Scripture: *"For the Lord GOD will help Me; therefore I will not be disgraced; therefore I have set My face like a flint, and I know that I will not be ashamed."* Isaiah 50:7

Ask God to help you as you work through this devotional study. Feel free to add to or change your answers at any time. You are encouraged to write all your answers.

1. During this week take some time to search your heart before God and discover what things may be distractions, hindering you from fulfilling God's purposes for your life.
2. Can you identify how you have been distracted from God's purposes in the past? What was/were the distraction(s)?
3. What made you realize you were being distracted?
4. How did you get back on track and what helped you overcome the distraction(s)?
5. Consider these Bible passages. Identify and record what distracted God's people from His purposes, how they became aware of the distractions, and what helped them get back on track.

Luke 9:51

Isaiah 50: 4-10

Luke 9: 1-6

I Kings 13:1-32

Luke 10: 1-20

Matthew 10: 5-42

6. Use a concordance if necessary or an Internet search engine and find some other Bible passages that highlight distractions, how they hinder the purposes of God, and how to get back on track after a distraction is recognized. Identify and write down what the distractions were that got the people off track with God, how they became aware of the distractions, and what helped them get back on track as expressed in each passage.
7. Ask God's help and try to find a few Bible passages that identify how something became a distraction to God's purposes. Write the references down and what caused the distraction each passage points to.
8. Have you noticed how someone close to you has become distracted from God's purposes for their life? How do you think it happened? How do you think the person can get back on track? Ask God to show you how to help them and intercede for them and do what the Lord tells you to do.
9. Ask God to show you how you can guard against distractions becoming a stronghold in your life, taking you away from the purposes of God. What has He shown you? Look for Him to show you what you can do to cooperate with Him as He purifies your heart.
10. Ask God to help you identify areas where you are vulnerable to distraction.
11. Choose one of the things God has shown you where you are being distracted or vulnerable to being distracted and work with Him in delivering you from it or preventing the vulnerability from becoming a distraction. Replace the distraction

or vulnerability by developing a godly habit to prevent your becoming distracted and incorporating it into your life. Input it into your mobile device or write it on a 3" by 5" index card and carry it with you. Review it several times a day. See how you do and chart your progress.

Recommended resources and/or projects for those who want to go deeper: Write a three-page essay about three major distractions in our culture that sidetrack Christians from God's best or prevent the lost from finding God. Explain how they are distractions and how they entrap people. Present a plan that you can use to help someone free a Christian from a distraction. Present a plan that you can use to help free a lost person who is distracted. Seek to put one of these plans into practice and document what happened.

11

Passive Adam or Proactive Jesus?

Do not merely listen to the word, and so deceive yourselves. Do what it says. James 1:22 (NIV)

"Men are from Mars and women are from Venus" as the saying goes. In a popular book by the same name the author describes gender-specific differences between men and women. Do we recognize these differences and adjust our communication style when talking to members of the opposite sex? If we are married, do we adjust our communication to fit the style and needs of our spouse?

If you are a man you have a choice of what kind of a man you want to be. Do you want to be passive like Adam or proactive like Jesus? If you are a woman these same principles apply to you as you decide whether to respond to life's challenges with passivity or with a proactive spirit. This devotional study should help you identify when these choices confront you and how to make the best response. Some times you should say and do nothing but pray. Other times you should speak out or take action. The most important thing is to walk close to the Lord, hear His voice, and follow Him (John 10:27).

Passive Adam or Proactive Jesus?

Let's first go to Genesis, chapter 3, and observe some characteristics of Adam in his relationship with Eve. God gave Adam the freedom to eat of every tree but the Tree of the Knowledge of Good and Evil and warned Adam of the consequences of eating from that tree. There is no record of God talking to Adam about the Tree of Life, the other tree in the midst of the Garden, before he and Eve disobeyed God. Adam and Eve could have freely eaten from the Tree of Life. It is not clear whether Adam warned Eve about the Tree of the Knowledge of Good and Evil but it is clear that she added another restriction which she attributed to God.

Some men, with a twinkle in their eyes, have referred to the woman as the "prime rib." They implicitly acknowledge the first woman was formed out of a rib from the first man and was extra special. Eve, like every wife, was meant to be held and protected, having a special place close to her husband's heart. She also had a natural sense of curiosity. Her unrestricted curiosity led to serious trouble. As the old adage says, "Curiosity killed the cat." We do well to learn from Eve's tragic mistake and limit our curiosity by restricting it to godly boundaries. We do even better to also learn from Adam's failure in his responsibility to love and protect Eve.

This account in Genesis also records how the tempter, Satan, in all of his cunning, laid a trap for Eve. It was also designed to ensnare Adam and bring all of the natural creation into bondage. In her curiosity, Eve was attracted to the one tree in the Garden that was off-limits for food, the Tree of the Knowledge of Good and Evil. She was wondering what made this tree different. What made this tree capable of producing death for her and for Adam?

At the opportune time, that old serpent stepped in and began to dialogue with Eve. Eve didn't realize she was in grave danger. Neither did Adam who remained silent at her side during the whole episode. As far as they were concerned, the subtle serpent was no more a threat than anything else God had created and put in the Garden. They didn't realize the serpent wanted to destroy them and reign in their place.

Satan appeared harmless as he questioned Eve about what God had said. Failing to recognize her danger by engaging in a dialogue with someone who questioned the Word of God was her first mistake. She let Satan set himself up as the expert who knew more than Adam and Eve about the tree and about God's motives. That was her second mistake. Satan deceived Eve into thinking God was withholding a good thing out of a desire to protect His superior knowledge. Very significantly, he also passed himself off as someone who had Eve's best interests at heart and acted like her friend. Adam did not speak the truth and warn Eve but allowed Satan's lies to take root by remaining silent. Adam remained passive and said nothing.

God did not warn Adam about touching the fruit but it appears He may have warned Eve. God created women to respond to touch. It can pull them in to doing things they will later regret. Eve examined this forbidden fruit and saw that it looked good to eat. She believed the serpent and wanted to be wise like God, knowing good from evil. She was enticed to violate her own conscience by touching the fruit as she picked some from the tree. Adam was watching but still said and did nothing. He still remained passive and didn't speak up and remind her of God's sober warning. Eve then violated God's specific command, ate of the fruit, and offered some to Adam. Passive Adam followed his wife in disobeying God's specific command and ate of the forbidden fruit.

It should be noted that this was the one and only restriction God had placed on Adam and Eve. God allowed this restriction to test their obedience and see whether they would believe and obey Him. They both failed the test and plunged into spiritual death and darkness. Immediately guilt, shame, and fear entered in. They quickly realized they had been "sold a bill of goods" and the serpent had lied to them.

Passive Adam or Proactive Jesus?

The fruit of the Tree of the Knowledge of Good and Evil was bitter indeed. Later, when God was walking in the Garden to fellowship with them, they ran and hid from Him as they trembled in fear and shame. This story clearly portrays the tragic consequences of Adam's inappropriate passivity.

Let's now take a look at the second Adam, the Lord Jesus Christ. Jesus was directly conceived by the Holy Spirit and remained the sinless Son of God. The Tempter came when Jesus was hungry, tired, and vulnerable to try to induce Him to sin but was met by stiff and immediate resistance. No passivity was found in Jesus. Jesus didn't focus on the temptation but He realized His real enemy was the devil. He immediately identified the lie — the "bill of goods" the tempter was trying to sell him. Then he promptly rejected it, quoting God's truth from the Scriptures. He followed the same method with each temptation. He knew and believed the Scriptures, relying completely on what God had said. Jesus passed the test with flying colors. He was ready for public ministry and left the desert in the power of the Holy Spirit.

If we want to be proactive like Jesus we do well to study His life and learn from Him. As we study the Scriptures, we can see Jesus was spiritually sensitive and well prepared for his encounter with the devil through a time of prayer and fasting. He had spent time alone with God in the wilderness. Jesus was also sensitive to the leading of the Holy Spirit as He was led into the desert to be tempted by the devil.

God led His only begotten Son into a time of testing when the time was ripe. The testing and tempting were done in private. Jesus had to pass the test before He was ready for public ministry. It is the same with us. God tests us in private so that our failures are not exposed to others for ridicule and so that others are not hurt by them. When we pass His time of testing, we are ready for public ministry and can be entrusted with the power of the Holy Spirit.

God has a way of preparing us for His purposes. It is through these wilderness times we learn how to recognize the Evil One and resist his lies. We may fail many of these tests repeatedly but God is patient and He continues to work with us. There is no shortcut for effective public ministry. We can and will take the test again and again, as necessary until we have established a track record of passing the test. Then God leads us to a place of fruitful ministry as we partner with Him. He also prepares future tests to enable us to be even more fruitful for Him as we embrace our God-given destiny.

The stakes are high but the rewards of successful obedience are great. The cost of failure to obey God is severe for us and for the ones we love whom we are called to protect. So are we going to respond to our situations in life as a passive Adam or as a proactive Jesus?

Chapter 11 – Passive Adam or Proactive Jesus

Pray, Study, Meditate, and Do

Key Scripture: *Do not merely listen to the word, and so deceive yourselves. Do what it says.* James 1:22 (NIV)

Ask God to help you as you work through this devotional study. Feel free to add to or change your answers at any time. You are encouraged to write all your answers.

1. During this week take some time to search your heart before God and discover where you have been passive when you should

have been proactive during a time when you or someone close to you was being tempted to disobey God.
2. Can you identify a time when you were passive and, as a result, someone close to you chose a path contrary to God's Word and both of you suffered for it?
3. Can you identify a time when someone close to you who cared about you was passive and, as a result, you chose a path contrary to the Scriptures and both of you suffered adverse consequences?
4. Can you identify a time when someone you cared about was about to violate God's commandment and you stepped in and warned them but they disobeyed God anyway? What were the consequences of their disobeying God?
5. Can you identify a time when you were about to violate God's commandment and someone who cared about you stepped in and warned you but you disobeyed God anyway? What were the consequences of ignoring the warning and disobeying God?
6. Consider these Bible passages. Identify and write down whether the person was passive or proactive in dealing with temptation and what the results were as expressed in each passage.

Genesis 3

Luke 4: 1-13

1 Samuel 13: 1-14

Exodus 32: 1-10

1 Samuel 24: 1-22

Exodus 32: 9-14

Galatians 2: 11-21

7. Use a concordance if necessary or an Internet search engine and find some other Bible passages that show a passive spirit when a person or a group of people were confronted with a certain temptation. Write down the references and identify what the temptation and response were and the consequences of the response chosen.
8. Use a concordance if necessary or an Internet search engine and find some other Bible passages showing a proactive spirit when a person or a group of people were confronted with a certain temptation. Write down the references and identify the temptation, the response, and the consequences.
9. Can you identify a time when someone you cared about was about to violate God's commandment and you stepped in and warned the person who then heeded the warning and didn't disobey God? What was the consequence of the person heeding your warning and obeying God?
10. Can you identify a time when you were about to violate God's commandment and someone who cared about you stepped in and warned you and you heeded the warning and didn't disobey God? What was the consequence of your heeding their warning and obeying God?
11. Identify some areas where you have been habitually passive and ask God to give you a plan to address them. Write them down and, with God's help, formulate and write down a plan to address them.
12. Choose one of the areas where you have been habitually passive and, with God's help, work on forming a new habit to be proactive. Input it into your mobile device or write it on a 3" by 5" index card and carry it with you. Review it several times a day. See how you do and chart your progress.

Recommended resources and/or projects for those who want to go deeper: Read a biography of someone who accomplished a lot for the Lord, such as Billy Graham or Paul Crouch. Read the story of the Apostle Paul in the book of Acts, chapters 8 -28. Note how they were proactive and not passive.

12

We Each Need a Vision of God to Endure

Where there is no vision the people perish. Proverbs 29:18a (KJV)

By faith he forsook Egypt, not fearing the wrath of the king; for he endured as seeing Him who is invisible. Hebrews 11:27 (KJV)

We all have difficulties in our lives and we often cope with them by trying to find a way to ease our pain. There are times when our personal world is being shaken and what worked for us in the past no longer works. When these times hit large segments of the population at the same time, many people lose their sense of direction and flounder around. I believe we are living in such times now where many of us have lost our sense of direction.

Often a clear sense of direction has all but disappeared during my times of personal shaking and uncertainty. The efforts I have put into my goals seem unfruitful. I may have also felt I have been drifting in my relationship with God. I have been going through such a season in the last several years since retirement. I have spent many hours watching TV and seen a lot of movies during this time. Sometimes I watch TV out of a sense of boredom. Other times it is to numb the pain caused by difficult circumstances.

I have wondered whether God has forsaken me or whether these fiery trials are designed to refine me. I know I am not alone in going through times like these and am aware of some of the trials others have been walking through. Have you, like me, also wondered, "What is the purpose of this trial?" Have you also experienced trials where apathy has replaced hope and you have a sense of hopelessness? Yet the Bible says, *"These three remain: faith, hope, and love. And the greatest of these is love."* 1 Corinthians 13:13

Let's look at the life of Moses, one of the heroes of the Bible, and see how he handled some of his trials. *"By faith he forsook Egypt, not fearing the wrath of the king; for he endured as seeing Him who is invisible"* (Hebrews 11:27). Moses did not have an easy life after killing the Egyptian and fleeing his home and privileged life to seek refuge in the desert. God provided for him and he raised a family during the forty years he spent as a shepherd in the wilderness. Then God revealed Himself to Moses, speaking through a burning bush that was not consumed.

God called Moses to go to Pharaoh, the "god-king" of Egypt, and persuade him to agree to let the Israelites go into the desert to worship Him. After enduring hardship and conflict with Pharaoh and calling forth plagues at God's direction, Moses participated with God in parting the waters of the Red Sea, allowing the Israelites to leave Egypt. Moses then spent the next forty years of his life leading the often rebellious and cantankerous Israelites through the desert while God prepared a new generation to possess the Promised Land. Moses endured because he saw God. He had a vision of God and he had an intimate relationship with Him.

The Bible teaches that God is no respecter of persons. We can learn some valuable lessons from Moses. Each of us needs to have a vision of God to endure. If we see God we will not lose hope because God is the source of all enduring hope.

If we have lost our vision of God, how can we reclaim it? If we have lost hope how can it be rekindled? A good place to begin is by examining our hearts to see whether they are pure. The Bible promises those with pure hearts are blessed because they shall see God (Matthew 5:8). To cultivate or restore a vision of God we may have to purify our hearts. Only God can give us a pure heart but we must consecrate ourselves and cooperate with Him in humble submission to receive it.

To see God accurately does not mean to see Him with our physical eyes. For God is a Spirit. The Bible makes it clear we cannot see God through the natural eyes. (*"But He said, 'You cannot see My face, for no man can see Me and live'"* (Exodus 33:20))! God is holy and we cannot get close to Him unless we are also holy. This kind of holiness is from the inside out and it is a work of God. As Hebrews 12: 14 puts it, *"Make every effort to live in peace with everyone and to be holy; without holiness no one will see the Lord"* (NIV).

Where can we find the strength to persevere through fiery trials, especially those that do not end quickly? I would submit that the Bible teaches we must have and maintain a vision of God to persevere.

What is a vision of God?

In *My Utmost for His Highest*, Oswald Chambers says in his May 9th selection, "There is a difference between an ideal and a vision. An ideal has no moral inspiration; a vision has." So a vision of God imparts a moral incentive for us. It is not the same as our conception of a perfect God. Our idea of God may even be accurate but it will not empower us to live a pure life. We need a vision of God, something that changes our hearts and souls.

Moses saw a burning bush and was open for God to speak to him. It changed his life and the lives of the children of Israel through his leadership. Saul was struck blind by a vision of God but it changed his life and resulted in a new name, Paul, and a transformed life. Paul's vision of God resulted in his missionary journeys and the writing of much of the New Testament. The twelve apostles also had a vision of God imparted to them through living with His Son, Jesus Christ, for three years. They had many moments of seeing God such as the time Jesus calmed the storm; the times He multiplied the bread and the fish to feed thousands; and the times he healed the sick, cast out demons, and raised the dead.

Seeing God must refer to having a perception of God's heart (seeing into God's heart). It does not mean seeing His face for He has said no one can look upon His face and live. So what is necessary for us to have a proper view of God? What distorts this view? A distorted view of God results when we have idols in our hearts. These idols prevent us from seeing God clearly and discerning His intentions. When our hearts are pure we are uncluttered by idols and the eyes of our hearts are able to see God.

So what is an idol? An idol is anything we hold onto that gets in the way of God and His purposes for our lives. It could be a person, a career, money, power, security, or any number of other things. In the final analysis, we either choose to follow God or we follow someone or something else. Perhaps the greatest idol we face is the idol of "self" – our desire to rule our own lives and our world in order to have our own way.

An idol may be recognized when we identify what consumes our lives and takes our focus off God. What is it that consumes our thoughts and seeks to be the main focus of our lives? Is it an idol? None of us are exempt from the pull of the desires of the flesh and of the soul that may become idols. Being controlled by fleshly appetites such as food or lust; soulish desires such as seeking entertainment or having an excessive focus on our appearance; or choosing to follow our own wills and living independently from God are all idolatrous manifestations.

> *"Do not love the world or the things in the world. If anyone loves the world, the love of the Father is not in him. For all that is in the world—the lust of the flesh, the lust of the eyes, and the pride of life—is not of the Father but is of the world. And the world is passing away, and the lust of it; but he who does the will of God abides forever." (1 John 2:15-17)*

Are you aware of any idols in your life? Are you willing to subject yourself to an examination of your heart by a holy God Who loves you dearly? The *Pray, Study, Meditate, and Do* portion of this devotional is designed to help you do just that!

Chapter 12 – We Each Need a Vision of God to Endure

Pray, Study, Meditate, and Do

Key Scriptures: *Where there is no vision the people perish.* Proverbs 29:18a (KJV)

By faith he forsook Egypt, not fearing the wrath of the king; for he endured as seeing Him who is invisible. Hebrews 11:27 (KJV)

We Each Need a Vision of God to Endure

Ask God to help you as you work through this devotional study. Feel free to add to or change your answers at any time. You are encouraged to write all your answers.

1. During this week take some time to search your heart before God and discover how you view God. Write down important details in your view of God.
2. Do you think you have an accurate view of God? Why or why not?
3. Has your view of God changed since you became a Christian? How did it change?
4. Can you identify what caused your view of God to change?
5. Consider these Bible passages. Identify the trial or hardship the people faced. Identify and write down how the people's view of God enabled them to endure as expressed in each passage.

    Daniel 6

    Daniel 3

    Acts 18: 9-10; 20: 17-38

    Mark 14: 16 – Mark 15:38

    Genesis, chapters 6 – 8

    Genesis 21: 1-21

    Genesis 22: 1-18

6. Use a concordance if necessary or an Internet search engine and find some other Bible passages that show hardships or trials facing different people and how their views of God helped them

to endure. Write down the references and identify the hardships or trials and how the people's views of God helped them endure as identified in each passage.

7. Ask the Lord to help you find several Bible passages that identify instances where people were unable to endure hardship. Can you identify what views of God may have been inadequate or inaccurate and contributed to them being unable to endure the hardships they faced?

8. Has your view or vision of God enabled you to endure hardships and trials? If your answer is "yes", describe your hardship or trial and how your vision of God helped you to endure it.

9. If your vision of God has been inadequate to help you through a trial or hardship, how was it inadequate? What do you think that tells you about your vision of God during that time of trial?

10. Are you aware of a time when there was an idol in your life? Reflect on that time and what made you aware you had an idol. How did you deal with it?

11. Are you aware of any current idols in your life? What are they? How did you become aware of them? Ask God to help you deal with them so they are no longer idols. What did God show you that would help you deal with any current idols?

12. Choose one of the things God has shown you that He doesn't want to continue to be a part of your life and, through seeking God and His help, work on removing its influence over you until it is no longer an idol. Input it into your mobile device or write it on a 3" by 5" index card and carry it with you. Review it several times a day. See how you do and chart your progress.

Recommended resources and/or projects for those who want to go deeper: the Book of Job in the Holy Bible. What vision did Job have and how did it help him endure. What caused Job to lose his faith and attack God's character to justify himself? How was Job's vision of God corrected or changed at the end of the Book of Job? Do you think Job would have been better equipped to go through his trial if he knew at the beginning of his trial what he learned about God at the end of it? If your answer is "Yes", in your opinion how would it have made a difference?

Overcoming Resistance from the Dark Side

Chapters 13-14

You are to be commended for every habit you have established as you worked your way through the first twelve devotional studies. Establishing twelve new habits into your character is the halfway mark for this course. The next two devotional studies are closely related and they will deal with hindrances from the devil and the demons that use the world to tempt the flesh. As we continue our journey, we must be properly trained and armed so we can identify, engage, and overcome these hindrances from the dark side.

It is also good to recognize the hindrances we face and overcome will continue to lurk in the dark and seek to take us off our chosen path throughout our lifetime on earth. We can never afford to just sit back and relax or take a spiritual vacation where we forget about God and His Word for a while. We can rest in Jesus and appropriate His victory in each area of our lives as we learn to fully trust and rely on Him for all things.

God will test us to see if we really believe Him and His promises. Sometimes things may look pretty dark for us as darkness closes in all around us as in this total eclipse of the sun. But Jesus is the Light of the world and He lives in us. He will break through all the darkness that temporarily hides His face from us. As we stand firm, the darkness will pass and the glorious Son will shine brightly in and around us.

13

RECOGNIZING YOUR ENEMIES

For we do not wrestle against flesh and blood, but against principalities, against powers, against the rulers of the darkness of this age, against spiritual hosts of wickedness in the heavenly places. Ephesians 6:12

If we cannot distinguish friend from foe we cannot engage our enemies or overcome them. The enemies of God and the Christian are usually grouped into three categories: the world, the flesh, and the devil (see 1 John 2:9-17). For instance, Satan and the demons steadfastly oppose God and war against the Christian. Yet people are not our enemies because we do not wrestle against flesh and blood (Ephesians 6:12). We also know the carnal mind (the flesh) and God's Spirit are irreconcilably opposed to each other (Romans 8:7-9). We need to recognize the unique characteristics of the world, the flesh, and the devil so we can distinguish them from each other.

The world or the cosmos is the world system that governs the minds of men and, through their minds, governs men. It is antithetical to the truth that comes through knowing Jesus and loving His Word. It includes the doctrine of evolution and the belief that the material world is all there is. It propagates the idea that man is the center of all things and that he can define good and evil. It has no place for God or divine revelation.

The flesh is the natural man cut off from the Spirit of God. When Adam and Eve committed the first sin in the Garden of Eden, their spirits died, cutting them off from God, the Source of life. They chose to partake of the Tree of the Knowledge of Good and Evil instead of the Tree of Life. The knowledge outside of God's will always leads to death. Knowledge imparted by God always leads to life. When we are ruled by our minds and mere human reasoning we are not ruled by the Spirit of God. Men without God are ruled by fleshly appetites and soulish desires – desires springing out of their own minds, emotions, and wills.

The third enemy is the devil. We use the term *the devil* collectively to include the demonic army ruled by the devil (Satan). This is an invisible enemy that torments us, oppresses our personalities, and attacks our bodies with sickness and disease. Satanic attacks come through thoughts and attitudes that deny God's truth, often introduced to us by the father of lies and his minions (see John 8:44). Their purpose is to entice us to act independently of God and contrary to His will. The sickness that attacks our bodies can also come from demonic sources.

However, Satan primarily works through deception. He deceives us into believing lies by projecting subtle distortions of the truth and using (faulty) human reasoning and circumstantial evidence or "facts." There is no room for faith or divine revelation when we allow ourselves to be led by Satan into deception. As the Holy Bible says in Romans 14:23b (NIV) "… everything that does not come from faith is sin." Now we will take a closer look at these enemies and how they work, starting with the devil.

Satan or the devil has many names in the Bible. His names reveal his character and tell us how he works. They include the adversary, the father of lies, the accuser of the brethren, the deceiver, the destroyer, and lord of the flies. He is characterized as a murderer from the beginning. Satan is devoid of good and truth. Deception is his specialty. He operates in the kingdom of darkness which encompasses all those who do not walk in the light of fellowship with God through trusting and obeying Him.

The kingdom of darkness is organized much like a government or an army. High ranking demons oversee different battlegrounds (Daniel 10:13-21) with lower-ranking demons under them (Mark 5:9). We know there are spirits of infirmity (Luke 13:11), as well as principalities, powers, and spiritual wickedness in high places (Ephesians 6:12). Every false religion has its origins in darkness (1 Timothy 4:1). We do well to recognize Satan and his legions as our enemies. They resist God and His will at every point and are enemies of all that is good.

It is of utmost importance to understand how Satan works against the Christian. The Apostle Paul writes: "Lest Satan should get an advantage of us: for we are not ignorant of his devices" (2 Corinthians 2:11; KJV). We are vulnerable if we are ignorant of "the wiles of the devil." Consider Ephesians 6:10-13:

> *Finally, my brethren, be strong in the Lord and in the power of His might. Put on the whole armor of God, that you may be able to stand against the wiles of the devil. For we do not wrestle against flesh and blood, but against principalities, against powers, against the rulers of the darkness of this age, against spiritual hosts of wickedness in the heavenly places. Therefore take up the whole armor of God, that you may be able to withstand in the evil day, and having done all, to stand.*

We will now take a closer look at another enemy, *the world*. It is based on human reasoning apart from divine revelation. It is opposed to God and is no friend of the Christian. It neither honors God nor does it submit to His laws. It is man-centered and has no room for God to play an active role. It rules mankind through people that use deception and intimidation. Psalm 2 reveals how all the rulers of the world band together to oppose the Lord and His rule.

The world system tries to push us into conformity with its values and is ruled by Satan (2 Corinthians 4:4). It follows the idea that man can be his own god and rule as he wishes. It allows man to replace God in defining right from wrong. Those who build their lives on this value system are building on sand. When the storms and floods come they will demolish the belief systems and foundations of those who built their lives on worldly principles and beliefs.

Those who believe the truth about Who God is and who they are in Him order their lives based on what God has said in His Word. They are careful to obey His commandments and are building on a foundation of solid rock, with Christ Jesus Himself as the Chief Cornerstone. When the storms and floods come, they will be left standing. What they build through partnership with God will withstand every onslaught against it. God uses them as He builds a temple of living stones, a house where He lives.

Next, we take a closer look at the third enemy of the Christian, *the flesh*. The flesh is perhaps the most insidious enemy of all. It can be referred to as the carnal mind or the fleshly nature. It is opposed to God's laws and is cut off from Him. It wants to replace God with "Self" as the ruler of the universe. Each man's flesh wants to rule over him and his world. It manifests in physical appetites and soulish desires of the mind, will, or emotions and makes no room for God.

If we are ruled by fleshly appetites such as food, drink, or sexual lust we are not being ruled by the Spirit of God. If we are ruled by soulish desires, we are not being led by the Spirit of God. We may pursue beauty, power, prestige, pleasure, the accumulation of material wealth, or other such things. These are soulish desires. Those who follow them are following the god of this world, Satan. He leads the natural man in the way he wants him to go through promising to satisfy his fleshly appetites and soulish desires.

Perhaps the greatest enemy of man is his own pride. Pride is often *the invisible sin* because those who have it the most are often least aware that they have it at all. God resists the proud and gives grace to the humble (James 4:6). We are exhorted to humble ourselves before the mighty hand of God (1 Peter 5:6). Then we can draw near to God and resist the devil so he will flee (James 4:7). Humility is the opposite of pride and is the cornerstone of a virtuous life. Pride is the cornerstone of an ungodly life.

Ungodliness may manifest itself in outwardly sinful acts and desires such as fornication, pornography, drunkenness, covetousness, theft, hatred, or murder. It can also manifest itself in self-righteousness, smugness, aloofness, judging others, or being a hypocrite. The words we speak are a good barometer for revealing what's in our hearts. Spending time with someone will reveal the type of person they are through what they say and do. Words, actions, checkbook registers, and credit card statements also reveal a lot about a person and their priorities.

God's solution for overcoming the world is to die to it and its pull on us. The apostle Paul said, "I am crucified to the world and the world is crucified to me" (see Galatians 6:14). Christian values and the world's values are mutually exclusive. Neither has any interest in the other and each pronounces the death penalty over the other. For example, Satan offered Jesus the kingdoms of this world if He would just bow down and worship him. But the Bible says:

> *Do not love the world or the things in the world. If anyone loves the world, the love of the Father is not in him. For all that is in the world—the lust of the flesh, the lust of the eyes, and the pride of life—is not of the Father but is of the world. And the world is passing away, and the lust of it; but he who does the will of God abides forever.* (1 John 2:15-17)

God's solution to the flesh is the death penalty. There is no way around it. We must face our need to die to the flesh and its pull on us. The apostle Paul said, "I have been crucified with Christ; it is no longer I who live, but Christ lives in me; and the life which I now live in the flesh I live by faith in the Son of God, who loved me and gave Himself for me." (Galatians 2:20)

The Bible gives us a sober warning about the lust of the eye, the lust of the flesh, and the pride of life. These are enemies of the purposes of God and must be recognized and faced. Jesus defeated them all when He went to the cross on our behalf and was crucified for our sins. His victories over the world, the flesh, and the devil have been imparted to us through what He did for us. His victory was complete as He rose from the dead, ascended to the Father, and is now seated on a throne at the right hand of the Father and His throne.

We were crucified with Christ, buried with Him, and raised from the dead with Him. We then ascended with Him and are now seated with Him. We must remember we are bought with a price and are not our own (1 Corinthians 6:20). Jesus purchased us with His blood. We are to glorify Him with our bodies and spirits which are His. It is our responsibility to renew our minds through His Word with the help of the Holy Spirit. Our sinful thought patterns and false beliefs need to be replaced with godly thought patterns and true beliefs based on God's Word as we learn to think in a godly manner.

Victory over Satan is also our inheritance from the Lord. When He died for us, we shared in His death. We also share in His life through His resurrection and ascension. We are now hidden in Christ and seated with Him in heavenly places at God's right hand — the position of greatest favor in the universe. As we learn to submit to God and draw near to Him, He will show us the things that hinder us from being one with Him and will enable us to turn from them. We will recognize the allure of the world and reject it. We will recognize the pull of the flesh and not respond to it. We will recognize demonic and satanic manifestations and wage successful warfare against these foes. Our victory is secured in Jesus's name through the power of His Holy Spirit.

Chapter 13 – Recognizing Your Enemies

Pray, Study, Meditate, and Do

Key Scripture: *For we do not wrestle against flesh and blood, but against principalities, against powers, against the rulers of the darkness of this age, against spiritual hosts of wickedness in the heavenly places.* Ephesians 6:12

Ask God to help you as you work through this devotional study. Feel free to add to or change your answers at any time. You are encouraged to write all your answers.

1. During this week take some time to search your heart before God and discover hidden enemies of your walk with God.
2. Can you identify two or three ways where Satan has worked against you and hindered God's work in your life? Describe what they were and how they hindered you.
3. Can you identify two or three ways where your flesh has hindered you from obeying God? Describe what they were and how they hindered you. What were the consequences?
4. Can you identify two or three ways where the world's values that oppose God have encroached into your values system and have hindered God's work in your life? Describe what they were and how they hindered you.
5. Consider these Bible passages. Identify who was hindered from obeying God and what the hindrances and adverse consequences were as expressed in each passage.

Judges 11

Daniel 10:1-14

Numbers 20:1-12

Genesis 4:1-16

Genesis, chapters 37, 39-41; 42:18-38; 43:3-9; 44:18-34; 50:15-21

Genesis 11:1-9

Genesis, 13:8-13; 14:8-17; 18:16-33; 19:1-38

Acts 5:1-10

1 Thessalonians: 2:18

2 Timothy 4:10

Acts 6:8-15; 7:54-60

Mark 6:14-29

Revelation 3:14-22

6. Use a concordance if necessary or an Internet search engine and find two or three other Bible passages showing hindrances to God's work through the devil's opposition. Write down the references and identify the key people involved, the hindrances, and their consequences.
7. Use a concordance if necessary or an Internet search engine and find two or three other Bible passages showing hindrances to God's work through the world's opposition. Write down the references and identify the key people involved, the hindrances, and their consequences.
8. Use a concordance if necessary or an Internet search engine and find two or three other Bible passages that show how God's people were hindered from obeying Him because of fleshly desires. Write down the references and identify the key people involved, the hindrances, and their consequences.
9. Give one or two examples where you recognized your enemy was Satan and you defeated him in his attempts to hinder you from obeying God. How did you recognize Satan was your enemy? How did you defeat him?
10. Give one or two examples where you recognized the world system was your enemy and you defeated its attempts to hinder you from obeying God. How did you recognize the world system was your enemy? How did you defeat it?

11. Give one or two examples where you recognized the enemy was your flesh and you defeated its attempts to hinder you from obeying God. How did you recognize the flesh was your enemy? How did you defeat it?
12. Ask God to help you to identify the areas where His will is being hindered in your life. Ask Him to help you identify your enemy in each case.
13. Ask God to show you where Satan has hindered you from obeying Him. Ask Him to show you how to win the victory over a specific area of hindrance from Satan. Write down what He shows you.
14. Ask God to show you where the world has hindered you from obeying Him. Ask Him to show you how to win the victory over a specific area of hindrance from the world. Write down what He shows you.
15. Ask God to show you how your flesh has hindered you from obeying Him. Ask Him to show you how to win the victory over a specific area of hindrance from the flesh. Write down what He shows you.
16. Ask God to show you one of the major hindrances from the world, the flesh, or the devil that has prevented you from fully obeying Him and commit to seek His will and follow His plan for defeating this hindrance. Commit to making victory over this hindrance into a habit you incorporate into your life. Input it into your mobile device or write it on a 3" by 5" index card and carry it with you. Review it several times a day. See how you do and chart your progress.

Recommended resources and/or projects for those who want to go deeper: *Daily prayer* from John Eldredge (https://www.ransomedheart.com/prayer/daily-prayer); *Daily prayer* (extended version) from John Eldredge (https://www.ransomedheart.com/prayer/daily-prayer-extended-version) © Copyright RANSOMED HEART MINISTRIES all rights reserved; *Preparing for War daily prayer* by Pastor Charles Stanley ©1988 (*Winning the War Within,* pp 123-125; Thomas Nelson Publishers).

14

How to Fight the Good Fight and Overcome Your Enemies

And they overcame him by the blood of the Lamb and by the word of their testimony, and they did not love their lives to the death. Revelation 12:11

Those who don't recognize their enemies will be overcome by them. They may be in many fights but they will usually not win. They will not land many punches because they will not know who to swing at. As we saw from the previous devotional study, enemies of the Christian can be grouped into three categories: the world, the flesh, and the devil.

Recognizing our enemies is an important first step but it is not enough to insure our victory over them. Those who haven't been trained in spiritual warfare and how to fight the good fight will be overcome. Those who go into battle without the proper protection (armor) will be wounded and defeated by their enemies. If we try to wage war against our enemies in our own strength and wisdom we will also be overcome.

How to Fight the Good Fight and Overcome Your Enemies

To be victorious we will need discernment, weaponry, a battle plan, and training in spiritual warfare – all provided by God. God has a plan for defeating every category of our enemies.

The Bible teaches us that we do not wrestle against flesh and blood (Ephesians 6:12). This means we must not see people as our enemies even though they may be controlled and used by our enemies to inflict great harm and maybe even the loss of life. Ephesians 6 talks about the armor of the Christian. We must wear our armor whenever we go into battle or whenever we can be attacked. This can be at any time. If we remove our armor, we will be vulnerable to attack and can be defeated. We must also learn to submit to God before we can successfully resist the devil so he will flee (James 4:7).

God has a different strategy for each category of enemies we face. We must discern the category of the enemy in each battle to use the proper strategy to defeat him. We cannot crucify the devil. We cannot fight against the flesh and resist it. We cannot focus on the darkness in the world and overcome it.

When we carry the light of God within us, it overcomes the darkness in the world around us. When the flesh wants to overcome us we must identify with Christ on the cross and crucify the flesh, making no provision for it. We must "cut off" thoughts that offend and "gouge out" ungodly desires that have been lodged in our hearts. We can successfully resist and overcome the devil as we learn to live by the Word of God (1 John 2:4). We should imitate Jesus and speak the truth out loud, if possible, when the devil plants a lie into our thoughts. When we are filled with the Word we will be made strong as we meditate on it and put it into practice.

As we learn to draw near and submit to God, we will put His will above our own will. We will choose Him above ourselves and our own desires.

We will learn to love Him with all of our hearts, souls, minds, and strength. We will become strong in the Lord and in the power of His might. When we are protected by the full armor of God and submitted to Him, He will enable us to stand even when the battle is fiercest. As we meditate on God's Word day and night, we make our way successful in God's sight (Joshua 1:8). We no longer seek the temporal pleasures of this world but our minds and hearts are set on things above where Jesus Christ is seated (Colossians 3:1-2). We are available and ready to be used by God at His pleasure.

We go to war with God in us and know it is He Who overcomes and not us. We follow His lead and walk in the victory He has won for us. We see ourselves as seated in the heavenly places in Christ Jesus where we exercise the authority of Jesus Christ Who grants all of our requests. This is because we ask according to His will, desiring only for the God and Father of our Lord Jesus Christ to be glorified.

Our minds are trained to recognize thoughts inconsistent with the truth of God so we can reject them, immediately replacing them with the truth from God's Word. We speak the truth in love. Our hearts are filled with love. Our minds are filled with truth. Jesus said, "Ye shall know the truth and the truth shall set you free" (John 8:32). Elsewhere it is written, "Your Word is truth." Jesus also says, "I am the Way, the Truth, and the Life. No one comes to the Father except by Me" (John 14:6). We also are quick to recognize and reject all idols. We must be strong in the Lord to fight the good fight and be victorious.

Knowing and keeping God's commandments make us strong and enable us to defeat God's and our enemies. (Deuteronomy 11:8). The verses below also include many practical steps to follow to help us keep God's Word as the focus of our lives.

> "Therefore you shall lay up these words of mine in your heart and in your soul, and bind them as a sign on your hand, and they shall be as frontlets between your eyes. You shall teach them to your children, speaking of them when you sit in your house, when you walk by the way, when you lie down, and when you rise up. And you shall write them on the doorposts of your house and on your gates, that your days and the days of your children may be multiplied in the land of which the LORD swore to your fathers to give them, like the days of the heavens above the earth.
>
> "For if you carefully keep all these commandments which I command you to do—to love the LORD your God, to walk in all His ways, and to hold fast to Him—then the LORD will drive out all these nations from before you, and you will dispossess greater and mightier nations than yourselves. Every place on which the sole of your foot treads shall be yours: from the wilderness and Lebanon, from the river, the River Euphrates, even to the Western Sea, shall be your territory. No man shall be able to stand against you; the LORD your God will put the dread of you and the fear of you upon all the land where you tread, just as He has said to you." (Deuteronomy 11:18-25)

God's plan for us can be found in Deuteronomy 10:12-22 and Deuteronomy 11. These verses emphasize the importance of loving God and obeying Him above all else. Consider Deuteronomy 10:12-13:

> "And now, Israel, what does the LORD your God require of you, but to fear the LORD your God, to walk in all His ways and to love Him, to serve the LORD your God with all your heart and with all your soul, and to keep the commandments of the LORD and His statutes which I command you today for your good?"

God gives us His commandments as a gift of love because they are for our own good. We also recognize God requires our wholehearted devotion. He is a jealous God and His purpose is to draw us into oneness with Himself. This means forsaking all idols and lesser loves when they conflict with the greatest love — the love for God Himself. Our wholehearted devotion is the best we can do but will never match the love of God expressed through Jesus dying on the cross. This is where the Father, the Son, and the Holy Spirit endured unfathomable separation and pain for our sakes. As we surrender fully to God, the love of the Trinity flows through us. We express the very love of God for God and for each other!

We must be strong in the Lord and not rely on our own strength. In humility, we must put on the full armor of God because Satan will attack and wound us in any unprotected area. We can be tripped up by deception if we drift away from the truth (our loins being girded with truth). Our hearts and our emotions will be vulnerable and can be wounded if we do not believe Christ is our righteousness (our breastplate of righteousness). We can lose our spiritual stability by not knowing who we are in Christ (the helmet of salvation). We must use our confidence in what God has said to repel the attacks against us (the shield of faith).

When we know God's Word and are yielded to His Spirit, the Sword of the Spirit will be our defensive and offensive weapon against the devil. If we do not keep our minds focused on Christ, trusting Him in every situation, we can lose our peace and be ineffective in spreading His "Good News," the Gospel of peace. Satan will attack us with subtle deceptions ("wiles") against our righteousness, our salvation, our faith, our truth, and our peace. We must be on guard and strengthen ourselves by feasting and meditating on God's Word to be victorious. ("I write to you, young men, because you are strong, and the word of God lives in you, and you have overcome the evil one." (1 John 2:14b; NIV)

Our greatest weapon is the Sword of the Spirit, the truth of God's Word, exercised in love as we walk in the Spirit. We know "love never fails." We love our neighbor as ourselves and we do not judge others. We discern their needs and petition God to meet them through our prayers. We war through intercession based on the wisdom and Word of God as the Holy Spirit leads us. We have overcome by the blood of the Lamb, by the word of our testimony, and we have not loved our lives unto death (Revelation 12:11). We lay down our lives for our brothers and sisters. We know we will participate in the resurrection of the just. God promises those who are faithful in a few things will rule over cities (Luke 19:17).

We will become one with the Father, the Son, and the Holy Spirit. We will be entirely filled with God and controlled by Him. His victory will be our victory. We will know when to be still and know that He is God. We will cease from our own striving and rest in His finished work on the cross. We will rest in the Father's love, knowing we are accepted in the beloved and well-pleasing in His sight. We will see ourselves as complete in Him. We will have all we need. Out of our innermost beings will flow rivers of living water which will serve to quench the thirst of those who cross our paths.

We will follow the Lamb wherever He goes. We will recognize this world is not our home. We will leave all to follow Jesus and will receive much more in this life and eternal life in the world to come. We will partake of the Marriage Supper of the Lamb for we are the Bride of Christ, a warrior bride, clothed in spotless garments of righteous deeds done out of a purified heart. We will be ready for the Bridegroom and ready to rule at His side with Him. Ours will be a glorious future. We will be among those who overcome as described in the Book of Revelation because we will be recognized as true disciples of Jesus Christ who overcome the world, the flesh, and the devil.

If we shrink back because of fear, God will have no pleasure in us. If we regard iniquity in our hearts, God will not hear our prayers. If we love the world and the things of the world, the Love of the Father will not live in us. If we follow deception, we will trip and fall. If we think we have no need for God or want to do things our way instead of God's way, we will be overcome. Those who have received Jesus as Savior but don't want to take up their crosses and follow Him will be saved but as those snatched out of the fire. All their works will be burned up (1 Corinthians 3:15).

God has marked out the path for the disciples of Jesus to follow. It is the path of the overcomer. Jesus asks, "Are you willing to follow Me?" Whether we overcome our enemies or are overcome by them is up to us and depends on our answer to this question. What will your answer be?

Chapter 14 – How to Fight the Good Fight and Overcome Your Enemies

Pray, Study, Meditate, and Do

Key Scripture: *And they overcame him by the blood of the Lamb and by the word of their testimony, and they did not love their lives to the death.* Revelation 12:11

Ask God to help you as you work through this devotional study. Feel free to add to or change your answers at any time. You are encouraged to write all your answers.

1. During this week take some time to search your heart before God and discover what spiritual battles you are engaged in.
2. Describe your spiritual armor and explain what each piece is designed to protect.
3. How does your shield of faith protect you? Give an example when it protected you and when you didn't use it and the consequences of not using it.
4. How does your helmet of salvation protect you? Give an example when it protected you and when you didn't use it and the consequences of not using it.
5. What does it mean for your loins to be girded about with truth? Give an example of when truth protected you and give another example when you failed to have your loins girded about with truth and what the consequences were.
6. How does the breastplate of righteousness protect you? Give an example of when the breastplate of righteousness protected you and give another example when you failed to have the breastplate of righteousness in place and what the consequences were.
7. Consider these Bible passages. Identify and write down the nature of the spiritual battle as expressed in each passage. Write down a key for a successful outcome or a key point of failure which led to a defeat for each passage. Think about how these principles would apply in your life with the spiritual battles you will face or are now facing.

Joshua 7: 1-25 (Israel fighting against Ai.)

Joshua 6: 1-21 (Israel fighting against Jericho.)

1 Samuel 14: 1-23 (Jonathan and his armor-bearer attacking the Philistines)

1 Samuel 17: 1 – 18:4 (David and Goliath)

Genesis 6: 1-7 (the Sons of God intermarrying with the daughters of men)

1 Samuel 2: 12-36 (Eli and his sons)

Mark 14: 66-72; Matthew 26: 33-35 (Peter denying Jesus)

8. Use a concordance if necessary or an Internet search engine and find some other Bible passages that show where Israel was successful in its warfare. Write down the references and identify the warfare and what contributed to victory from a spiritual perspective in each reference.
9. Ask God to lead you to a few Bible passages identifying where Israel was defeated in a battle. Write the references down and what contributed to Israel's defeat from a spiritual perspective.
10. What does it mean to have your feet shod with the preparation of the gospel of peace? Can you give one example when your feet were shod and another example when they were not? What were the consequences in each instance?
11. The sword of the Spirit is the only offensive and defensive weapon. How do you use the sword of the Spirit which is the Word of God? Can you give examples of when you used in properly and when you didn't and what the consequences were?
12. Do you always wear each piece of your spiritual armor? Ask God to show you a few things you can do to improve your readiness for battle through the way you wear your spiritual armor.
13. Choose to strengthen a weakness God has shown you to help you fight the good fight and, with God's help, work on making it a habit that you incorporate into your life. Input it into your mobile device or write it on a 3" by 5" index card and carry it with you. Review it several times a day. See how you do and chart your progress.

Recommended resources and/or projects for those who want to go deeper: Read from *Acts* Chapters 8 – 28, focusing on the apostle Paul, his spiritual warfare, and how he overcame. Write some keys that led him to victory in his spiritual warfare. Study the apostle Judas in the Gospels and write the key reasons why he failed and his life ended up in a great tragedy.

Overcoming the Pull of the Flesh

Chapters 15-18

You have now identified fourteen habits you want to establish through relying on God and His strategies, power, and plans. How is your success rate? Although this course has a timeline to follow, you can choose your own timeline. God will continue to work with you and help you all the days of your life. This next section returns to the struggle we have within as a result of our own fallen nature often referred to as *the flesh*. The flesh has its own appetites and wants to do its own thing, only thinking about itself. If we are going to become mature disciples of Jesus Christ, we cannot let it have its way and must learn to habitually deny it. We will be exploring hindrances from the flesh and how we can overcome them in the next four chapters.

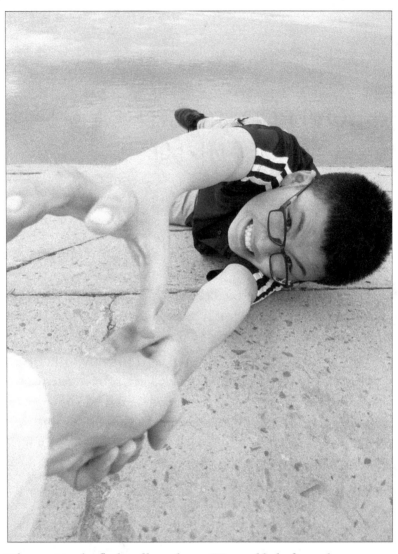

Like gravity, the flesh pulls us down. We need help from above to overcome. God is our Helper. He uses His Word, His Spirit, and His people to help us in our time of need. All we need to do is reach up to Him in faith. He will never let us go.

15

YOUR FOCUS FACTOR

"But seek first the kingdom of God and His righteousness, and all these things shall be added to you." Matthew 6:33

Have you heard of the Platte River in Nebraska? It is a broad meandering river that was first discovered by French explorers and fur trappers in the early Seventeenth Century. It is only inches deep and is a tributary of the Missouri River which, in turn, is a tributary of the powerful and important Mississippi River. The Platte River has almost no power and is of limited usefulness because of its shallowness. Contrast that to today's technology that enables us to perform delicate operations and shoot down guided missiles through focused laser beams. Laser technology has the remarkable ability to focus rays of light into a very powerful and narrow laser beam. In a similar way, a magnifying glass can start a fire by focusing the sun's rays into a tiny point. These two illustrations demonstrate the importance of focusing available resources.

As has been said, the mind is a terrible thing to waste. A well-educated mind is a visa to an almost limitless future. But a mind requires a will to focus it and wisdom to focus it on the right things. If we want a bright future we must develop the ability to focus our minds on the right things. The *right things* are the most important things–the things of the greatest strategic importance, not only for our lifetimes but for all of eternity. Out of His great love for us, God instructs us how to focus our minds on the right things. God instructs us through the Holy Bible to bring every thought captive to Christ. We are not to set our minds and hearts on earthly things but on things above (Colossians 3:1-2) where Christ Jesus is seated at the right hand of God, the Father.

Experience confirms that when our hearts are set on one thing it is hard or impossible for us to focus our minds on another thing. The heart must be set first. The right focus for the heart and mind is Jesus Christ Himself. Focusing on Jesus draws us closer to Him which is what He wants. In addition, when He and what is important to Him is the focus of our affections and our minds, we are ready to be directed by Him into a life of maximum fruitfulness for God and His kingdom.

Faith in God and His Word are prerequisites for developing the right focus. How do we develop a proper focus? It begins by realizing we were crucified, buried, and raised with Christ and are now seated with Him in heavenly places at the right hand of God, the Father Almighty. Having our values aligned with God's values is necessary if we are to realign our priorities to match His priorities for us. Jesus said, "Seek first the kingdom of God and His righteousness and all these things will be added to you" (Matthew 6:33). When we put God and His kingdom first, He takes care of us, gives us what we need, and usually much more. This is how we enter into the abundant life Jesus promised.

How do we keep our hearts and minds from becoming divided? The key is to cultivate focusing our minds and hearts on Jesus Christ and not allow ourselves to be distracted. We must have an eye focusing on what is good because we will go in the direction of our focus. We must control our thoughts or they will control us. When we lose our focus, we lose our ability to follow Christ closely. We also lose our ability to rise above the circumstances.

Consider Simon Peter, a disciple, and apostle of Jesus. He walked on water when he kept his focus on Jesus. When he allowed himself to be distracted by the circumstances of the raging storm with its strong winds and high waves, his mind was overcome through his senses. Fear was stirred up within him and he lost his faith, sinking below the waves. Jesus pulled him up out of the water and saved him when he cried out in desperation. Then Jesus asked him the pointed question, "Why did you doubt?"

As it was with Peter so it is with us. We lose our focus by allowing circumstances and distractions to take our eyes off Jesus. Then our hearts and minds can be pulled in other directions and we begin to doubt God's Word and His promises. When we lose our faith in God and His promises, we are overcome by circumstances and flounder in our walk with Him.

We must focus on the positive instead of the negative, on finding solutions instead of the problems. Jesus is and has the solution to every problem. Because God is light and Jesus is the Light of the world, we must focus on light. Because God is love, we must have our hearts focused on love. We can choose our own focus. We can choose to focus on the negative things people say, on the difficulties of our circumstances, or on Jesus and the promises He gives us.

When we focus on the good and speak positive things, we feel better. When we focus on what does not seem good and speak negative things, we feel worse. We eat from the fruit of our lips, whether the fruit is good or bad (Proverbs 18:20-21). Our feelings are controlled by what we believe to be true. For example, a little boy who is undergoing surgery and is having infection cut out to save his leg will feel pain. If he doesn't understand why the surgeon is doing this, he will think the surgeon is hurting him. However, a seasoned soldier who is having gangrene cut out of his leg will feel pain just as the little boy did. But he will be grateful and thankful if he focuses on how the surgeon is saving his life and his leg which will heal.

Consider what happens when we speak. We must first think about what we say. Next, we say it. Then we hear it. Then it rolls around in our mind for a while. That's a lot of reinforcement! Let's keep our focus on whatever is pure, lovely, just, and of good report. As we think about these things we will learn how to walk above the circumstances instead of being overcome by them.

At times we will find it necessary to cut off wrong thoughts from our minds and gouge out evil desires from our hearts. I believe this is what Jesus was getting at when He talked about cutting off your hand or gouging out your eye if it offends you (Matthew 5:29-30). The problem is not with the hand or the eye. The problem is with what we allow in our minds and hearts. The next example applies specifically for men but the principles can be applied more broadly for anyone.

In the book, *Every Man's Battle,* Fred Stoeker and Stephen Arterburn talk about the battle men have with lustful thoughts and behavior toward women. Many valuable insights are shared such as bouncing our eyes when we see an object of lust such as an immodestly dressed woman. *Bouncing your eyes* means to *immediately* turn them elsewhere. Dealing with our thoughts is also discussed. When we train our eyes and minds to respond to what is good and to avoid what is evil, our minds then form a consensus of what is *allowable* and what is *not allowable*. A well-trained mind screens out those things which are not allowable subconsciously. This helps us avoid temptation.

The Old Testament character Job was the most righteous man in his day. He said. "I made a covenant with my eyes. So why then should I think upon a maid" (see Job 31:1)? I believe the takeaway for us is to first learn the habit of controlling our eyes before we tackle the more difficult task of controlling our thoughts. By making a covenant with our eyes we do not allow ourselves to look at objects of lust. Keeping this covenant with our eyes provides momentum for us to keep lustful thoughts from gaining a foothold in our minds. We can tell ourselves that since we are not going to *look* upon (covet) a woman lustfully it makes no sense to *think* lustfully about one either. The covenant with our eyes helps us to control our thoughts. It works like judo where we use the momentum already created through our covenant with our eyes to defeat the lustful thought.

I do not wait for a temptation to present itself. I am proactive and positive in my approach by filling my mind with God's Word. God gave me a particular Scripture to help me in this area. When tempted, I may say it several times out loud or under my breath: "Blessed are the pure in heart, for they shall see God" (Matthew 5:8). The joy of the promise and fulfillment of seeing God is so much greater than the temporary pleasure of lust for a season. The Lord may have a different Scripture for you. Just ask Him.

As we learn to focus on Jesus, we become more like Jesus. Let us consider Him and make Him the focal point of our hearts, minds, eyes, and lives.

Chapter 15 – Your Focus Factor

Pray, Study, Meditate, and Do

Key Scripture: *"But seek first the kingdom of God and His righteousness, and all these things shall be added to you."* Matthew 6:33

Ask God to help you as you work through this devotional study. Feel free to add to or change your answers at any time. You are encouraged to write all your answers.

1. During this week take some time to search your heart before God and discover the *focal points* for your life, those areas where portions of your life are centered.
2. Does your life have one main focus? If so, what is it?
3. Do you have difficulty maintaining your focus? Can you identify what causes the difficulty?
4. What do you think your main focus should be?
5. Consider these Bible passages. Identify and write down the main focus of the person or people as expressed in each passage, whether they were distracted from God's purposes, and, if so, what was the main distraction.

2 Samuel 11 (David and Bathsheba)

2 Kings, chapters 18-19 (King Hezekiah)

1 Kings 3: 4-15 (King Solomon)

John 20: 24-29 (Thomas, the apostle)

Numbers, chapters 22-24 (Balaam and Balak)

John 3: 23-36 (John the Baptist)

Judges 4:4 – 5:31 (Deborah the Prophetess)

John 20: 1-18 (Mary Magdalene)

6. Use a concordance if necessary or an Internet search engine and find some other Bible passages focusing on advancing God's kingdom. Write down the references and identify their focus.
7. Ask God to help you find two or three Bible passages that identify distractions from God's main focus. Write down the references and distractions.
8. Do you have a strategy to deal with distractions? What is it? How well does it work?
9. Does God have a strategy to deal with distractions? What is it? Have you tried it? How well has it worked for you?
10. Ask God to show you a few things you can do to help you keep your focus on Him and His purposes for you.
11. Choose one of the things God has shown you and work on making it into a habit and incorporating it into your life. Input it into your mobile device or write it on a 3" by 5" index card and carry it with you. Review it several times a day. See how you do and chart your progress.

Recommended resources and/or projects for those who want to go deeper: *Acts* Chapters 8 – 28: Consider the Apostle Paul and how he kept his focus on what was most important. Also, consider the distractions he had. Recommendation for men: *Every Man's Battle* by Fred

Stoeker and Stephen Arterburn. This book focuses on how to win the war against lust.

16

THE IMPORTANCE OF DISCIPLINE

But I discipline my body and bring it into subjection, lest, when I have preached to others, I myself should become disqualified. 1 Corinthians 9:27

Have you ever thought about the resistance one must overcome in order to accomplish anything? I have. Consider houses, cars, clothes, works of art, earned degrees, roads, bridges, and anything else man has made. When we reflect on the work required to build, make, or accomplish such things we realize focused sustained effort is always necessary. We also recognize we don't always *feel like* doing worthwhile things. If we simply follow our feelings, tasks requiring a steadfast resolution to finish will never get done. Even small projects require a certain amount of discipline to finish.

King Solomon, known for his extraordinary wisdom, stresses the importance of discipline in the first chapter of Proverbs. These phrases show his emphasis: "for attaining wisdom and discipline" (v. 2), "for acquiring a disciplined and prudent life" (v. 3), and "fools despise wisdom and discipline" (v. 7). Since discipline is associated with wisdom and a prudent life and lack of discipline is associated with being a fool, embracing discipline is essential for living a productive life.

In another context, we see discipline from another perspective. An ancient Chinese proverb says, "The longest journey begins with the first step." But many more steps are necessary to complete the journey. So it is with worthwhile goals. To accomplish them requires maintaining our focus on our goal. We see this all the time in the sports world, no matter what the sport. Longer-term goals require workable plans to reach them. Complex goals are more easily achieved by breaking them down into simpler intermediate goals with associated plans.

To reach our goals we must marshal our resources to focus on our objective with sustained effort. This applies even when we enjoy what we are doing. Sometimes the effort is a joy and other times it seems like drudgery. When you are in love, the work you do for your beloved may seem almost effortless. But in our rough-and-tumble world, many mundane and necessary tasks may seem more like drudgery. The important thing to remember is we must overcome distractions and resistance to accomplish our goals. Without discipline, this would not be possible.

Discipline requires having discernment and exercising our wills to bring our minds, bodies, and other necessary resources into service to accomplish the objective. We may be required to say *no* to hunger pangs, fleshly desires, and contending thoughts or activities that would distract us from moving toward our goal. We must also evaluate our thoughts, desires, and actions and prioritize them based on whether they will help or hinder us from reaching our goal. Experience shows it is good to develop sufficiently detailed plans to reach both original and subordinate goals. Initially writing down our plans and periodically reviewing them will help us keep focused on our objective and resist *the wandering mind* syndrome.

We must also discipline ourselves to not let our emotions or appetites rule over us. Discipline is also needed to not let harmful or unfruitful thinking rule over us. Having a clear vision of our goals and engaging our imaginations will help us to formulate realistic plans to reach them. When you write down your goals and plans, be sure to include a timeline for achieving them. This will help you keep on track. Ideas without realistic plans for implementing them are just fantasies. Plans without necessary resources are incomplete and cannot be fully implemented. Plans without a timeline for implementation will likely not be executed satisfactorily and may not be executed at all.

The main hindrance to discipline is our flesh. Our fleshly or carnal self-centered desires will ride roughshod over us and others if we let them. The Bible says we are not obligated to the flesh to fulfill its sinful desires (Romans 8:12). Our victory comes by truly believing our old nature was crucified with Christ and reckoning ourselves dead to sin (Romans 6:11). We must not allow fleshly impulses to rule us but bring every thought into subjection to Christ (2 Corinthians 10:5). Jesus overcame all evil thoughts. Because I am a new creation in Christ, I rely on His victory over them as I look to Him in faith. The Bible teaches we are servants to that which we obey (Romans 6:16). If we yield to fleshly appetites we become their servant. If we yield to distractions we become their servant. We are to set our hearts and minds on things above and not on the things of this world (Colossians 3:2). When we fail, we can confess our sins to God, receive His forgiveness and cleansing, and get back on track.

Sometimes it takes great sustained effort over a long period of time to accomplish a significant and important goal. The pyramids were not built in a day. President John F. Kennedy's vision to send a man to the moon and back also took many years to fulfill. It may take a lifetime or more to complete something God has put on our hearts. But without the discipline to hold us to the task, we are prone to give up when the going gets tough. Flexibility may also be necessary. Are we willing to make adjustments if our current plans prove to be unworkable? If we are guided by wisdom in setting and implementing goals, discipline will see us through.

Making disciples of Jesus Christ also requires discipline and takes time and sustained effort. It requires identifying goals and breaking them down into steps, making detailed plans to achieve them. Much more important, it requires us to be led by the Spirit and obedient to God's Word. As we engage in the discipleship process, our thoughts, beliefs, actions, and habits will be changed over time to conform more closely to those of Jesus Christ. We can share with others what has helped us obey the commands of our Lord as we learn to follow Him more closely. We must work together and follow the lead of the Father, the Son, and the Holy Spirit to make disciples of all nations and help fulfill the Great Commission.

Changing a culture or a society can be a monumental task, but it can be accomplished through sustained effort over several generations if necessary. Change can be for good or for evil, for better or for worse. Discipline is a double-edged sword that can be used for good or evil purposes. Sadly, our culture has been in decline because those with evil intent had goals and plans and the necessary discipline to carry them out. As Christians, we are called to be salt and light. We are to preserve, season, and enlighten our culture. We must be prepared to be *poured out of the salt shaker*. For us to accomplish our mission, we cannot afford to lag behind the ungodly in developing a disciplined life. We have the Holy Spirit and the Word of God to help us.

Be mindful that perseverance is a character quality God wants to build into our lives. Remember not to be too quick to give up if you encounter resistance. Discipline your thoughts, actions, and habits and you will increase your success. Pay attention to what is going on around you to see if you have to adjust your plans. Don't ignore or delay addressing small problems that may lead to bigger problems if neglected. We should always pray for wisdom because we need it and because God encourages us to ask Him for it. "But if any of you lacks wisdom, let him ask of God, who gives to all generously and without reproach, and it will be given to him." (James 1:5; NASB)

The cost of negligence and procrastination is best illustrated in this famous quote:

> "For the want of a nail, the shoe was lost.
> For the want of a shoe, the horse was lost.
> For the want of a horse, the rider was lost.
> For the want of a rider, the battle was lost.
> For the want of a battle, the kingdom was lost,
> And all for the want of a horseshoe nail."
> — Benjamin Franklin

The importance of developing good habits and unlearning bad habits cannot be overestimated. Both require discipline. Repetition of thoughts creates habits. Established habits become part of our character. Our character affects others for good or for bad. Developing and maintaining a holy and godly character will have a profound effect on others that come into your life. God wants us to be holy. He wants us to partner with Him in building holiness into our character.

> *"For I am the Lord your God. You shall therefore consecrate yourselves, and you shall be holy; for I am holy. Neither shall you defile yourselves with any creeping thing that creeps on the earth. For I am the Lord who brings you up out of the land of Egypt, to be your God. You shall therefore be holy, for I am holy."* Leviticus 11:44-45

Pursue peace with all people, and holiness, without which no one will see the Lord. Hebrews 12:14

Chapter 16 – The Importance of Discipline

Pray, Study, Meditate, and Do

Key Scripture: *But I discipline my body and bring it into subjection, lest, when I have preached to others, I myself should become disqualified.* 1 Corinthians 9:27

Ask God to help you as you work through this devotional study. Feel free to add to or change your answers at any time. You are encouraged to write all your answers.

1. During this week take some time to search your heart before God and discover where you lack discipline and how it is hindering you in reaching your full potential for God.
2. Can you identify an area where you are well disciplined and how it has helped you?
3. Can you identify an area where you lacked discipline in the past and how it has hurt you?
4. Can you identify some areas where you used to lack discipline but now are well disciplined? What motivated you to change and how were you able to change?
5. Consider these Bible passages. Identify and write down where discipline is shown or lacking and what the results were as expressed in each passage.

The Importance of Discipline

1 Kings 11:1-13

Judges 14: 1-3

1 Kings 11:26 – 39

1 Samuel 25:2-42

2 Samuel 11:2-27

Genesis 39:6-10

Daniel 6

Acts 5:1-10

Genesis 13:1-13; 19:1-38

2 Samuel 15:1-37; 18:9-15

6. Use a concordance if necessary or an Internet search engine and find some other Bible passages showing the importance of discipline and the blessings of being disciplined. Write down the references, the discipline shown, and the results of that discipline. Be specific.
7. Ask God to lead you to find a few Bible passages identifying a breakdown in discipline and its consequences. Write down the references, where the breakdown of discipline occurred, and the adverse consequences it caused.
8. Do you remember a time when your discipline kept you from a harmful choice and consequences you would have regretted? What discipline kept you from making the harmful choice?

What was the choice? What consequences would you have regretted?

9. Do you remember a time when you lacked discipline in a certain area and, as a result, you made a choice you have regretted and have suffered adverse consequences? What were the lack of discipline, the choice, and the adverse consequences?
10. Can you think of benefits resulting from positive patterns of discipline in your life? What were the positive patterns of discipline and what were the benefits?
11. Choose one area God has shown you where you would benefit from having additional discipline and, with God's help, work on disciplining that area and incorporating it into a habit. Input it into your mobile device or write it on a 3" by 5" index card and carry it with you. Review it several times a day. See how you do and chart your progress.

Recommended resources and/or projects for those who want to go deeper: *Making Good Habits Breaking Bad Habits* by Joyce Meyer (Faith Words)

Do a character study of Abraham in *Genesis* and see how his loyalty to God played out and how his unwillingness to stand up for his wife played out. Research the high cost to King David and Israel because of his undisciplined lust, resulting in adultery and murder.

17

OVERCOMING INERTIA AND GOAL SETTING

"But seek ye first the kingdom of God, and his righteousness; and all these things shall be added unto you."
Matthew 6:33 (KJV)

I spent a good amount of time in my early retirement years just *drifting with the tide*. I did not have a fixed schedule to keep or heavy responsibilities requiring a lot of time. This is not necessarily a bad thing. We may remember God instructed the Israelites to let the land lay fallow for one year out of seven. No crops were to be planted so the land could replenish itself with nutrients necessary to support productive crops. Similarly, we may need a time of diminished responsibilities for personal restoration. As my Dad used to say, "All work and no play make Jack a dull boy." In moderation, rest and relaxation are good but excesses lead to deterioration in our personalities and a loss of focus and productivity.

One way of avoiding low productivity and excess drifting with the tide is to make a habit of setting your own realistic goals. It will help you make the best use of your time and resources. I have found it helpful to do my thinking with a pad and pen for writing down my ideas. A survey of Harvard Business School MBAs, taken several years after they graduated, showed the most successful were those who developed the habit of writing down their goals. One author recommends writing down three goals to accomplish each day. Focus on the goals. Allow plenty of time for interruptions and other things. Don't write down too many goals or you may become discouraged if you fail to accomplish some of them. If you can't accomplish all of your goals for the day, write down the unfinished ones as part of your plan for the next day.

Our goals should relate to important areas of our lives and they should address the different needs we have based on the season of life we are in. We should include spiritual, mental, social, physical, financial, family, job-related, church-related, and community-related goals. Christians should understand God wants first priority in our lives so we should have a plan to spend quality time with Him on a daily basis. We should give God all the time He needs so He can do what He wants with our lives. Spiritual goals should include time for Bible reading, prayer, and meditation. They may also include ministries God puts on our hearts such as teaching a Sunday school class, visiting with the elderly, or making a meal for someone who is incapacitated. Financial goals should include a plan to get out of debt and a plan to save for long-term financial needs such as buying a house or funding a retirement nest egg. It can also include a plan to further the education of someone in your family to enable them to qualify for a more enjoyable or higher paying job.

We may have heard the popular saying: "Failing to plan is planning to fail." If we don't plan anything for the day, we may go into *default mode* which may include watching several hours of TV, being on the Internet for several hours, and eating too many snacks. Default mode may be fine for a little downtime but is it good stewardship to continue in this vein for long periods of time? You can never go back and relive yesterday.

The best we can do is to learn from our mistakes or the mistakes of others and not repeat them. We don't have to drift into an unmotivated, unfulfilling, unproductive or slothful life. I've been there. I've done that. I don't want to go back there. It is better to find a suitable part-time job, take up a hobby, or do volunteer work to help others. That's one reason why I've taken up writing.

We have four seasons in a year and we know each season has its own particular requirements and appropriate work. Similarly, our lives also have different seasons. God allows us to do some things for a season but seasons change. It is good to recognize when our season is changing. We shouldn't try to continue to do something for one season of our life when it no longer fits the new season we are in. If we put God first in our lives, remembering He is a jealous God, He will let us know when to lay down one activity and when to pick up another one. He is the Equipper and the Preparer and He knows what is best for us. Let us learn to follow His leading instead of setting ourselves up as the rulers of our own lives and the masters of our own destinies.

It is good to have goals and to set other goals as we realize our lives are changing. It is good to think of different goals to help us accomplish worthwhile things in our lives based on our current and anticipated future seasons. These goals should have different timelines. Some may be accomplished in a few minutes or in an hour. Others may take a week or two, or even several months. Longer range goals may take a year or more such as earning a certificate or a college degree while others may take perhaps forty years to accomplish such as accumulating the wealth necessary to retire comfortably.

The best motivator for setting and accomplishing goals is love. Love does not think selfishly but does not neglect itself either. It maintains a healthy balance. Physical goals may include a daily exercise routine to include working out at a gym three times a week. It is wise to choose activities to accomplish multiple goals such as adding a social goal to your exercise goal by inviting someone to join you for a workout at the gym or your daily walk. Younger people can schedule basketball games, swimming, jogging, or other sports as enjoyable activities enhanced by doing them with others.

Friendships are a necessary part of life and we must take time to develop and maintain them. They won't develop without making them a priority and having plans to nourish them. Married couples are benefited by planning a weekly date with their spouse. This is a good idea even if you have young children. It will help *keep the home fires burning*. These dates should focus on quality time which can be more important than quantity time. They should include activities that energize both spouses.

Civic duties and service to the community are also areas where goal setting is helpful. Seek the Lord as to how He may want you involved in your community. You may want to help someone with godly values and character in their campaign for an elected office. You may do a fundraiser, help them by making phone calls, write letters-to-the-editor, put up signs, or talk to your friends and acquaintances about why you think they would be a good fit for a particular office. Make sure you register to vote and take the time to find out about where the candidates stand on important issues. Consider their track record and preparation for the position, as well as their character, vision, and plans to accomplish what they are promising the voters.

Take an hour or two on a regular basis to review your life and where it is going. See what is missing. Look at what works and what doesn't work for you. Eliminate time wasters and energy drainers and look for other ways to meet your needs and the needs of those you love. You will discover those who plan their lives effectively are more highly motivated in life and have a better quality of life. As Christians, it stands to reason we will be better stewards of our lives as we seek godly wisdom and the

Holy Spirit's guidance in making plans for our future. Isn't that what you want for yourself and for your loved ones?

Go ahead and make my day! Join me in setting some meaningful goals!

Chapter 17 – Overcoming Inertia and Goal Setting

Pray, Study, Meditate, and Do

Key Scripture: *"**But** seek ye first **the kingdom of God, and his righteousness; and all these things shall be added unto you.**"* Matthew 6:33 (KJV)

Ask God to help you as you work through this devotional study. Feel free to add to or change your answers at any time. You are encouraged to write all your answers.

1. During this week take some time to search your heart before God and discover some areas of your life that would be benefited by setting meaningful goals.
2. Can you identify something you would like to change in a key relationship that would be benefited by setting a goal? Ask God to help you identify a goal and give you a plan you can implement that will improve this relationship. Write it down and, after you have implemented it, document how your relationship improved.

3. Can you identify a financial need where setting a goal and implementing a plan will facilitate meeting it? Write down your financial need, your goal, and your plan. Document the results.
4. Can you identify a spiritual need where setting a goal and implementing a plan will facilitate meeting it? Write down your spiritual need, your goal, and your plan. Document the results.
5. Consider these Bible passages. Identify and write down a key need, a goal, and a plan to satisfy the need as expressed in each passage.

    Genesis 6:13-22

    Genesis 41: 33-36

    1 Chronicles 29: 1-9; 2 Chronicles 2:1-18

    Ruth 3:1-5

    Genesis 24:1-67

    Titus 1: 5-9

    Matthew 14: 13-21

    Exodus 16: 4-6

    Matthew 28: 18-20

    Matthew 6: 33

6. Use a concordance if necessary or an Internet search engine and find some other Bible passages, identifying important needs and people's attempts to meet them. Write down the references

and identify needs and attempts to meet them as identified in each passage.

7. Search for some Bible passages identifying plans and goals to meet important needs where those involved went outside of God's will while trying to meet them. Write the references down and the associated needs, goals and plans. How did they go outside of God's will and what was the result?
8. Have you ever tried to meet an important need through a plan outside of God's will for your life? What was the need? What was the plan? What was the result?
9. Have you ever tried to meet an important need by asking the Lord to show you how to do it and studying His Word for an answer? What was the need? What was the plan? What was the result?
10. Ask God to show you a few areas where you have important unmet needs and what He wants you to do to meet them. Write down the needs, goals, and plans to meet them. After implementing the plans go back and document the results in your electronic device or notebook. This will build your faith.
11. Choose an important need God has shown you and seek Him for a plan to enable you to meet it in a godly way and implement the plan. Input it into your mobile device or write it on a 3" by 5" index card and carry it with you. Review it several times a day. See how you do and chart your progress.

Recommended resources and/or projects for those who want to go deeper: *The Purpose Driven Life* by Rick Warren (Zondervan)

18

MAINTAINING YOUR BALANCE

And Jesus grew in wisdom and stature, and in favor with God and man. Luke 2:52 (NIV)

I remember when I was first learning how to ride a bike. I needed a little help to get going. Being instructed was not enough. I also needed a push. But I seemed to aim at every garbage can on the street when I wanted to slow down or stop. More than a few neighbors yelled as I crashed into their garbage cans. But before too long I learned how to steer, stop, and maintain my balance. My bicycle did not have training wheels so I had to learn the hard way.

Have you ever learned how to ride a bicycle? Do you remember how difficult it was to stay on the bike? It was much easier to stay on it when you were peddling and moving if you were doing a good job steering. The key was to maintain your balance. This is true in both the natural and spiritual realms. When someone is losing their balance they must regain it quickly or they will fall.

We juggle home and family responsibilities with work obligations. Then throw in church and community commitments along with citizenship responsibilities. And of course, we have to fit in time with God. The pressure of too many responsibilities and not enough time can be very intense during certain seasons of our lives. It is not easy to maintain our balance between home and work, work and school, church and home, and everything else we try to fit into our schedules. What's a Christian to do?

Then there is the problem of energy. Can we find the energy to fulfill our obligations and desires and the needs and desires of those close to us? Work can be draining and family conflicts can especially take away our energy. If we have health issues our energy is further drained. If we are caring for an aged parent, a chronically ill child or spouse, or if we are in some other high-demand caregiving role, we can easily become too drained to take care of ourselves. Can we recognize our limitations and distinguish between those tasks we must personally do and those we can delegate; between what is really necessary and what is optional; and between what can and cannot be postponed? The time will come when we will have to learn how to say "No!" when asked to do something or to take on another responsibility because we will not have the time or the energy.

We also need balance in how we handle our finances. Should we get a new dishwasher and postpone a much-needed family vacation? Should we buy a new home to better meet the needs of our growing family and hold on to our seven-year-old car for a couple more years? Should we get high-speed Internet service, cell phones, or cable TV instead of saving the money toward a college education for our children? Should we support the missionary from our church or should we give to the evangelistic association that reaches out to people in crisis? Should we buy our clothes at the local Goodwill store so our teenage daughter can buy a new outfit from the upscale department store? Should the husband take an extra job to pay for the optional utilities and family vacations? Should the wife find a full-time job to replace her part-time one and find a babysitter for the kids? There are many financial decisions to make in the course of a lifetime. Each will require wisdom in balancing limited resources to best meet our needs.

Multitudes are in the valley of decision and you and I are among them. We've considered balancing time, energy, and financial resources among contending demands or requests for them. Let's now consider questions about personal choices. Is it OK for me to indulge my sweet tooth, have a beer or two with the guys, or have a glass of wine to help me relax in the evening? Is it OK to smoke a daily cigar or to go through a pack of cigarettes every few days when they seem to calm my nerves and help me relax? Should I practice portion control to cut down on my calories or should I avoid the weekly buffets and eat more salads instead? Do I need a gym membership or will I have the self-discipline to work out at home if I buy some exercise equipment? Do I really need seven to eight hours of sleep per night or is the current six enough? Do I need to take prescription drugs to help me with my anxieties, depression, or mood swings? The questions are almost endless but we all need to consider what is best for our bodies and souls as well as our spirits. The more important question may be: How can we live a balanced life? Let's examine this further.

Several years ago I had a dream about a strong man who was dressed like those who work in a circus. He had a barbell of heavy weights which he could easily lift because of his great strength. The challenge he faced was to pick up the heavy barbell and carry it across a tightrope without losing his balance and falling. How could he do this? It seemed pretty impossible to me. Then I saw him climb up the ladder with the barbell and lift it straight up over his head and quickly walk across the tight rope. He had plenty of strength to lift the heavy barbell and, by lifting it directly over his head, he maintained his balance. I sensed the Lord had a message for me through this dream and He wanted me to share it with others.

When I asked the Lord about the dream, I sensed He was saying the secret of maintaining balance with our responsibilities (heavy weights) is more than just maintaining a strong body, mind, and spirit although this is essential. We must also lift our burdens to the Lord (straight up over our heads) and allow Him to carry them and give us what we need when we need it. He will show us what to do and how to do it. This is what the Bible teaches as shown in these passages:

> *Give your burdens to the LORD, and he will take care of you. He will not permit the godly to slip and fall.* (Psalm 55:22; NLT)

> *In every place of worship, I want men to pray with holy hands lifted up to God, free from anger and controversy.* (1 Timothy 2:8; NLT)

Living a balanced life requires wisdom. God promises to provide this when we ask in faith, without doubting. A balanced life is a life submitted to God and to His rule. It cannot be achieved by mere human effort. Yet we must live responsibly and not neglect our duties. We cannot be passive and wait for God to do everything. The balance must be achieved between what we are to do and what we are to trust God to do. We cannot take on His responsibilities and He will not exempt us from doing ours. It is a partnership with God where He gives us the grace to do all we should do as we humble ourselves before Him and trust Him to do what we cannot do.

We will learn more about how we can live a balanced life before God as we engage in the *Pray, Study, Meditate, and Do* portion of this devotional study. Are you ready to proceed?

A DISCIPLE'S JOURNEY

Chapter 18 – Maintaining Your Balance

Pray, Study, Meditate, and Do

Key Scripture: *And Jesus grew in wisdom and stature, and in favor with God and man.* Luke 2:52 (NIV)

Ask God to help you as you work through this devotional study. Feel free to add to or change your answers at any time. You are encouraged to write all your answers.

1. During this week take some time to search your heart before God and discover weather your life could be better balanced.
2. Can you identify the key components of a person's life that should be balanced?
3. Can you identify any areas of your life that are out of balance?
4. Do you know anyone who seems to have a well-balanced life? What makes it well-balanced?
5. Consider these Bible passages. Examine the person in each reference below and write down what makes their life balanced or unbalanced as expressed in the passage.

Apostle Paul – Col. 1:29, Phil. 4:13

King Saul – 1 Samuel 10:15-16, 20-24; 15:1-31

Nabal – 1 Samuel 25:2-39

Mary, mother of Jesus – Luke 1:26-56

> Mary's husband, Joseph – Luke 2:4-52; Matthew 1:18-25; 2:13-23
>
> Apostle Thomas – John 20:24-49
>
> Moses – Exodus 18:13-26
>
> James, the Lord's brother – Acts 15:13-29; Galatians 2:9; James 2:14-26

6. Use a concordance if necessary or an Internet search engine and find some other Bible passages that give examples of or instructions in creating or maintaining a balanced life. Write down the references and identify what you think are the key elements of a balanced life in each passage.
7. Ask God to lead you in finding some Bible passages that identify unbalanced lives. Write the references down and the imbalance(s) they point to.
8. Can you name two or three areas in your life that seem out of balance? What are they?
9. In your opinion, if you feel your life is a little out of balance, what is the main area to balance? If your life seems well-balanced, explain why.
10. Ask God to show you a few areas in your life where some adjustments could be made, resulting in a better-balanced life. Ask Him to guide you in identifying the adjustments and ask for His help in making them.
11. Choose one area needing change and work on making the necessary adjustments into a habit so you will be a better-balanced individual. Input it into your mobile device or write it on a 3" by 5" index card and carry it with you. Review it several times a day. See how you do and chart your progress.

Recommended resources and/or projects for those who want to go deeper: Consider watching the *Star Wars* Trilogy paying attention to the training and practice for a Jedi master. How could a spiritual application or adaptation of Jedi training be applied to a Christian? Have you learned anything from these movies that could be applied to your life to make you a better-balanced Christian?

The Seven Habits of Highly Effective People by Stephen Covey

Help from High Places

Chapters 19-22

If you have established seventeen new habits at this point in our studies you are to be highly commended. It is not an easy feat. If you relied only on your own strength you would not have been successful. God has given us a Helper, the Holy Spirit, and His Word to provide the strength and wisdom we need. He will bring us into maturity as we trust Him. The next four chapters of this course explore some of the ways God wants to help us as we gain more insight into His Word and character.

Although it is not apparent on earth, Jesus is now reigning from heaven as the Lion of the tribe of Judah in full submission to His Father. While He was on earth, He was in full submission to His Father as the Lamb of God to take away the sin of the world. We are to walk in His footsteps as we follow Him. We are to be in full submission to Him as the lambs of the Good Shepherd. We will also reign with Him for eternity and are to bring the kingdom of heaven to earth as we pray and add feet to our prayers.

"Thy kingdom come. Thy will be done on earth as it is in heaven."
(Matthew 6:10; KJV)

19

GOD'S LAW AND GRACE

"You shall have no other gods before me." Exodus 20:3 (KJV)

Have you ever wondered how God's laws relate to the Christian under the New Covenant? Are they to be totally disregarded, meticulously observed, or treated in some other way? This is a very important question. Historically, professing Christians have believed from one extreme to the other. But what does the Bible teach?

Do we seek to earn or maintain God's acceptance and favor through keeping the law? The Apostle Paul warned those who teach this doctrine preach another gospel and are under the strongest condemnation (Galatians 1:6-9; 2:15-16). Other Christians think God's laws are no longer important. But Jesus said, "Whoever therefore breaks one of the least of these commandments, and teaches men so, shall be called least in the kingdom of heaven; but whoever does and teaches them, he shall be called great in the kingdom of heaven" (Matthew 5:19). King David was a man after God's own heart and I believe he had the right perspective. He loved God's law, constantly meditated on it, sought to obey it, and understood its benefits (see Psalm 119).

The law requires us to love God supremely and to love our neighbor as ourselves (Matthew 22:36-40). Jesus kept God's laws perfectly because He walked in perfect love, fulfilling all the requirements of the law (Romans 13:10; Galatians 5:14). It was love that brought Jesus to the cross where He paid for our sins. Because of love, Jesus's righteousness is credited to us when we turn to Him in repentance and faith. Because of love, God sees us clothed with the righteousness of Christ and hidden in Him. Although keeping God's law doesn't save us, our failure to keep it shows there is something missing in our walk with God. What's lacking is love (Galatians 5:13-14).

Through His love Jesus says, "I kept the law for you. Now I want to keep the law through you. Then others will see Me in you. Allow Me to work My love in you so you love God, your neighbor, and yourself as I do. When My love flows and shows through you, others will be drawn to Me and My Father will be glorified."

God expects us to learn to walk by faith. Yielding to Jesus allows Him to keep God's moral laws through us. This is the true covenant of grace where we exchanged our old life for the new life of the resurrected Christ (Philippians 1:21a). The power of the Holy Spirit within us enables us to obey God. As we learn to walk in the Spirit by faith, we will grow in our ability to keep His commands. We will fail if we try to keep them through our own efforts.

We will now turn our attention to examine the heart of God's moral laws as codified in the Ten Commandments. They were written on two stone tablets kept hidden inside the Ark of the Covenant. This symbolized the law was to be kept hidden inside every believer's heart. The Mercy Seat was over the Ark. This symbolized God made provision for His mercy to cover our failures.

God's Law and Grace

God also promised to put His law in our minds and write it on our hearts (Jeremiah 31:31-33), indicating He did not expect us to do it on our own. We are responsible to renew our minds through meditating on and obeying God's Word as we are enabled through trusting Jesus. This ensures our prosperity and success in all that we undertake (Joshua 1:8). This is one reason Christians need to pay attention to God's laws.

God also works through order and priorities. He reveals His order and priorities through His creation and the Holy Bible. He revealed law before He revealed grace. The original covenant (Old Testament) was based on a relationship with God and His people through His laws. It pointed to the coming of the Messiah and a better covenant with better promises. This new covenant (New Testament) was made between God and His Son, the second Adam. God's blessings were earned by Jesus Who perfectly kept God's laws and purchased His bride with His blood. Jesus makes His blessings freely available to all who believed in and received Him as Savior and Lord.

God already sees us as justified and hidden in Christ, covered by His perfect righteousness, when we first accept Him. However, God's laws are like a mirror. They show us our current level of sanctification. Exposure to God's laws reveals our sin but they don't change us or clean us up. Sooner or later, we recognize we can't keep God's holy laws. Through faith we look for Christ to do this in us just as we turned to Him in faith to save us.

God first uses the law to motivate us to recognize our need for a savior. Then He reveals His grace to show us how He wants to free us. This is how He works in us to prepare us to open our hearts and minds to seek and find the Savior. The law's function is to take us by the hand and lead us to the Savior, the Master Teacher. Then Jesus saves and teaches us, changing us in the process. (See Romans 7 and Galatians 3:21-25.)

We are God's priority. He gave His commandments to guide and bless us because He loves us. The rest of this study focuses on understanding and applying God's priorities through the Ten Commandments to our lives. They are the foundation of God's moral laws and we don't apply them to be justified but to be blessed and to be drawn closer to Jesus. You are encouraged to read the full text in Exodus 20:1-21 before proceeding.

Bible teachers, pastors, and scholars have pointed out the first four commandments focus on man's relationship with God and the last five focus on man's relationships with his fellow man. The fifth Commandment is a "swing commandment" and transitions from focusing on honoring God, our heavenly Father, to honoring our earthly father and mother. Let's look at the Ten Commandments to discern what they say about God's order of priorities and how we can apply them to our lives.

The Ten Commandments

1. "You shall have no other gods before me."

God deserves and requires a unique and supreme position in our lives above everyone and everything else. This is the First Commandment. The verse is also translated as "You are to have no other gods *besides* me" (Deuteronomy 5:7; ISV). The First Commandment establishes God's place as central to our hearts and lives. "You must worship no other gods, for the LORD, whose very name is Jealous, is a God who is jealous about his relationship with you" (Exodus 34:14; NLT). He is the only One we are to worship. We are also to love Him supremely. Jesus stated this same priority in what has become known as the Greatest Commandment (Matthew 22:37). Deuteronomy 6:4 also emphasizes this priority. When we understand Who God is and how much He loves us, we would gladly only worship Him and love Him supremely.

2. "You shall not make for yourself an image in the form of anything in heaven above or on the earth beneath or in the waters below. You shall not bow down to them or worship them…"

The Second Commandment says we are not to create our own image of God. We are not to worship or honor any man-made image of God. What we create is never to be in competition with the God Who created us. Even our own theology is not to be unduly honored or worshipped. As the Holy Bible says about God, "I am Who I am." We cannot put God in a box, control, or define Him. He is far greater than our minds or abilities to grasp Him. He is to be worshipped, not controlled or defined. Obeying this commandment keeps us from idols.

3. "You shall not misuse the name of the Lord your God, for the Lord will not hold anyone guiltless who misuses his name."

Although we cannot create an image of God, He does have a name. He has actually revealed Himself through several names. Each name reveals different aspects of His character. His primary Old Testament name is Jehovah or Yahweh. His name is to be honored and not treated as common or profane. If we misuse His name we dishonor Him and He will hold us accountable. In the New Testament, we learn Jesus is also God and the name of Jesus is given special honor. Only in Jesus's name are salvation, healing, and deliverance. His name also gives us access to God for answered prayer. "And I will do whatever you ask in my name, so the Father may be glorified in the Son." (John 14:13; NIV). To honor God's name is to honor Him. To dishonor His name is to dishonor Him and there will be consequences. Jews didn't even mention His name as it was regarded as too holy to even speak it.

4. "Remember the Sabbath day by keeping it holy."

The Fourth Commandment tells us we are to set aside one day a week to focus on our special relationship with God and to renew our bodies, souls (mind, will, and emotions), and spirits. We are to refrain from the normal activities of labor requiring *the sweat of our brow* and have a day of rest, refreshment, and restoration. God set the example when He worked six days and rested on the Sabbath (seventh) day.

Because He made us in His image, we are to follow His example and also rest one day out of seven. Obeying this commandment requires us to trust God to provide for our physical needs through six days of work instead of seven. Although the New Testament gives us liberty in this area (Romans 14:5), our personal convictions may require us to oppose our employer and culture if we are being required to work on Sunday or for seven days a week on a regular basis. Jesus said, "The Sabbath was made for man, not man for the Sabbath" (see Mark 2:27; NIV). Working seven days a week on a regular basis without taking time for rest and worship will take its toll. It will likely lead to a state of exhaustion or burnout. We can trust God to guide us and provide for us in any situation where we seek to honor Him.

There is a deeper spiritual application for this commandment as revealed in the New Testament: When we have entered into God's rest we are at a place where we have ceased from our own labors (see Hebrews 4:10). This is not associated with a particular day but with entering into a place where we cease from our own labors and rest in Christ. Then we are no longer trying to work for God but we are cooperating with God and allowing Him to work through us.

5. "Honor your father and your mother, so you may live long in the land the Lord your God is giving you."

The Fifth Commandment is also referred to as the first commandment with a promise (Ephesians 6:2). As we examined the first four commandments we see they relate closely to the Greatest Commandment. The last six commandments relate closely to the Second Greatest Commandment.

> *Jesus replied: "'Love the Lord your God with all your heart and with all your soul and with all your mind.' This is the first and greatest commandment. And the second is like it: 'Love your neighbor as yourself.' All the Law and the Prophets hang on these two commandments."* (Matthew 22:37-40; NIV)

To give honor to someone is to prefer them above yourself. It is to give deference to the other person. It is an expression of humility where we esteem others above ourselves. Our parents deserve a special place in our hearts and lives as they have given us life in this world and have nurtured us, however imperfectly. It is rare to find anyone more committed to you than your parents whose image and likeness you bear. God promises to honors those who honor their parents by giving them a long and satisfying life.

6. "You shall not murder."

On the human level, the first and foremost prohibition God gives is the wrongful taking of human life – murder. When you take a person's life, you take away their future and everything they have on earth. Human life is a higher priority than health or possessions and is to be given the greatest protection under our laws. When someone strikes against a human being they strike against the image of God in man and against

God Himself. They are saying, "We will not have this Man to rule over us." (Luke 19:14; BSB)

Many of us are living under an unspeakable tragedy that has been going on for far too many years. This is the tragedy of abortion. In 1972, the U.S. Supreme Court presumed to create a right for a mother to abort her baby. Killing babies in the womb actually deprives them of their inalienable right to life as recognized by the U.S. Declaration of Independence. What this Supreme Court did create was a tragedy, resulting in the deaths of tens of millions of developing human beings. Other countries have done similarly.

Abortion is the wrongful killing of human life and regarded by God as sin. The Scriptures show John the Baptist and his mother, Elizabeth, both recognized Jesus as Lord shortly after He was conceived. John the Baptist, conceived six months earlier, "jumped for joy" in the womb when Mary entered the room. And Elizabeth, under the inspiration of the Holy Spirit, addressed newly-pregnant Mary as "the mother of my Lord" when she entered the room (see Luke 1:39-45). These and other Scriptures reveal God confers personhood upon conception.

Maybe you or someone close to you have had or caused an abortion. There is no reason to despair under a burden of genuine guilt. Jesus came to take your guilt, shame, sin, and its punishment and give you His righteousness and a new life in Him. He shed His blood to pay for all of your sins. He can and wants to forgive even those who took the life of an unborn baby, whether done with both eyes open or in ignorance. Confess your sin to Him and grieve over what you have done but let Him heal you. Receive His forgiveness and know God will take care of the baby. No matter how hard it is to do, you must also forgive yourself.

7. "You shall not commit adultery."

The foundation for a stable society is a stable marriage. God intended a child to be conceived, protected, and provided for by a father and mother. It is the oldest institution God created and the most important one to be protected. Just as destroying life is forbidden by God so is doing things to destroy a marriage. Committing adultery was punishable by stoning in the Old Testament. It is also the only sin Jesus recognized as grounds for divorce.

In the Sermon on the Mount, Jesus expanded on adultery to include lusting after a woman in your heart. Based on His statement, men who view pornography are committing adultery in their hearts and need to repent. Most men have done this some time or another. As Scripture says, "all have sinned, and come short of the glory of God" (Romans 3:23; KJV). Confessing your sin to Jesus and repenting of it is the means to be cleansed of this destructive habit. Jesus died so you could be set free from the bondage of all sin. Turn to Him in faith and trust Him to lead you into the freedom He purchased through His blood.

The physical act of adultery results in destroying unborn babies, children, adults, marriages, souls, and society. Although many of its consequences cannot be reversed, those who have committed adultery may repent and receive God's forgiveness. He will take away the sin, guilt, shame, and pain. You must also forgive yourself and embrace the new life He gives you in Christ. That is your identity now.

8. "You shall not steal."

Those who steal show they value something more highly than they value a relationship with God. This is idolatry and forbidden by the First Commandment. Coveting must also have existed before the stealing occurred. This violates the Tenth Commandment. When you steal, you hurt your neighbor and do not love your neighbor as yourself. You violate the Golden Rule, "Do unto others as you would have them do unto you." You could steal a life or steal a wife. These are dealt with in the Sixth and Seventh Commandments. Your decision to steal will harm your neighbors and may result in someone's loss of possessions, health, livelihood, or life.

9. "You shall not give false testimony against your neighbor."

Giving false testimony can destroy someone's reputation. Lying in court can result in harm to the one you're falsely testifying against or to the victim when you are protecting the perpetrator of a crime. It contributes to a miscarriage of justice if the judge or jury relies on your testimony. It also separates you from God because it is sin. You fail to love God and to love your neighbor as yourself when you give false testimony against your neighbor, violating the two greatest commandments.

10. "You shall not covet your neighbor's house. You shall not covet your neighbor's wife, or his male or female servant, his ox or donkey, or anything that belongs to your neighbor."

Those who covet want for themselves what belongs to someone else. It's a sin to desire what is not yours to have. Be satisfied with God and what He has provides for you. Don't desire what belongs to someone else. Also remember the promise that God will withhold no good thing from those who walk uprightly (see Psalm 84:11b).

Your heart wants to steal when it covets. Coveting separates you from God and from others. You desire to enrich yourself at the cost of impoverishing your neighbor. When things become more important than God, you are making them into an idol, breaking the first and second commandments. Remember, "The LORD gave, and the LORD has taken away; blessed be the name of the LORD." (Job 1:21b)

Brief Summary of the Ten Commandments

1. Worship God alone by putting Him first in your heart and life.
2. Don't create or honor any man-made gods. Don't let anything come before you and the Lord your God. Don't let anything compete with God.
3. Revere and honor God's name. This includes Jesus's name.
4. Honor God's Sabbath day by setting it apart as a time of rest and worship. Trust God and rest in His provision for you instead of striving to do it all yourself.
5. Honor the parents God gave you. He used them to give you life and raise you. Your father and mother are a reflection of God, the Father, and the Holy Spirit who nurture and guide you.
6. Do not wrongfully take a human life which was made in the image of God.
7. Do not steal another's intimacy or spouse as it destroys souls and marriages.
8. Do not wrongfully take possessions belonging to another.
9. Do not use the law by bearing false witness against your neighbors to deprive them of what is rightfully theirs including their reputation.
10. Do not set your heart on what belongs to someone else.

Guiding Your Priorities through the Ten Commandments

Top Five Priorities toward God

1. Worship God alone
2. Don't allow anything in your life to compete with God
3. Protect God's name and reputation through your words and deeds
4. Honor God's day and trust Him to provide for your needs

5. Honor God by honoring your parents

Top Five Priorities toward Man

1. Protect lives
2. Protect marriages
3. Protect property rights of others
4. Protect reputations by telling the truth
5. Rejoice in what God has given others

Chapter 19 – God's Law and Grace

Pray, Study, Meditate, and Do

Key Scripture: *"You shall have no other gods before me."* Exodus 20:3 (KJV)

Ask God to help you as you work through this devotional study. Feel free to add to or change your answers at any time. You are encouraged to write all your answers.

1. Have you ever thought God's moral laws didn't apply to you because you were under grace? Do you remember breaking any of them? Do you see how they apply to you now? Where does grace fit in?
2. Do breaking God's moral laws have consequences even if you are a Christian and under grace? Have you experienced consequences for breaking any of them? What was the law and what were the consequences? Where does grace fit in?

3. What is the difference between punishment and discipline (see Psalm 59:5; Hebrews 12:4-11)? Does justice require punishment? Does love require discipline? Was Jesus disciplined or punished on the cross? If you are on the receiving end, can you always tell the difference between punishment and discipline based on how it affects you at the moment? If you are a Christian and understand God loves you will He discipline or punish you?
4. Do you remember thinking you had to keep God's laws or He would punish you? When you didn't keep God's law did He punish you? Did He discipline you? What is the key in knowing whether you are being disciplined or punished?
5. Have you ever felt that God turned His back on you because you sinned? Do you think you felt this way because you believed your relationship with God was based on your keeping God's laws instead of being justified freely by His grace? What happened to make you feel better about your relationship with God? Where does grace fit in?
6. If you fail to keep a moral commandment what does that tell you about your "love walk"? Examine one of your past moral failures and see if you can trace it back to the point where your love toward God and your fellow man broke down. Describe the incident and write down your analysis and conclusion.
7. During this week take some time to search your heart before God and ask Him to show you how you can better order your life using the Ten Commandments as a guideline.
8. Can you identify any idols or other gods that sometimes take God's place in your life?
9. How can you tell whether you have an idol in your life?
10. Can you identify ways people misuse or abuse God's name, taking it in vain? Have you ever abused or misused God's name? What brought it on? What would have been a better response that would have honored God?

11. Consider these Bible passages. Identify and write down which commandments were broken, who broke them, and how they were broken as expressed in each passage.

    Exodus 32:1-10

    Genesis 31:30-37

    Genesis 27:1-45

    Genesis 37:17-36

    Nehemiah 13:15-22

    Genesis 19:15-26

    2 Timothy 4:10

    2 Samuel 11

    2 Samuel 3: 12-34

    2 Samuel 13: 23-38

    Acts 17:16-34; 19:23-41

    Acts 7:51 – 8:1

    Joshua 7

12. Use a concordance or an Internet search engine if necessary and find some other Bible passages that show God's commandments being broken, why they were broken, who broke them, and what

the consequences of breaking them were. Write down the references and your answers.

13. Ask God to lead you to Bible passages identifying tests where God's people were tempted to break one or more of His commandments. Write the references down and what commandments the people were tempted to break. Write down key circumstances composing the test and how the people responded.
14. If you think about it when you break any of the commandments you automatically break one or two other commandments. Can you identify which commandments these are and why they would also be broken?
15. Why was it important to keep the Sabbath day? Is it still important today? Why or why not?
16. Do we still make idols or "graven images" today? What are some of the most common idols in our modern culture? Are any of them an idol for you? If so, how should you biblically deal with it?
17. How do people commit adultery today? What are some of the consequences? In light of what Jesus said about committing adultery, what are some other ways people commit adultery today? Have you committed adultery? How do we deal with the consequences of committing adultery and how can we be restored in our relationship with God?
18. What cultures in the world today show a high honor for parents? How can we honor our parents? What dishonors our parents? Have you ever dishonored your parents? How? How did you feel? How did it affect your walk with God? How were you restored?
19. What does it mean to covet? What are some common forms of coveting today? Have you ever coveted? How? What were your consequences from coveting? How did it affect your walk

with God? How were you restored? What did you learn from the incident?

20. Is the commandment to not bear false witness against your neighbor equivalent to not lying? Why or why not? Is it ever right to lie? Give scriptural justification for your position.
21. Can you think of a time when you stole something? What did you steal? How did you feel? What were the consequences? How did it affect your walk with God? How did it affect your walk with the person you stole from? How were you restored? What did you learn from the incident? Is it possible to steal non-material things? Give an example.
22. Choose an area where you have been having trouble keeping one of God's commandments. Ask Him to show you how you can better keep that commandment. Write down what He shows you and work on making the necessary changes to consistently keep that commandment. Input it into your mobile device or write it on a 3" by 5" index card and carry it with you. Review it several times a day. See how you do and chart your progress.

Recommended resources and/or projects for those who want to go deeper: *America, Garden of the Gods* by James Robison

20

CHECKING YOUR PROGRESS THROUGH THE BEATITUDES

Now when Jesus saw the crowds, he went up on a mountainside and sat down. His disciples came to him, and he began to teach them. (Matthew 5:1-2; NIV)

We explored God's law and grace and how to apply God's priorities as expressed through the Ten Commandments to our lives in the last devotional study. Now we will turn our attention to what may be the most revolutionary teaching in history, the *Sermon of the Mount*. *The Sermon on the Mount* was addressed to Jesus's disciples. We will focus on the Beatitudes because they are signposts, marking progress for disciples on the road to maturity. These guidelines will help us know where we are and what to expect as we continue to follow Jesus. The Beatitudes, given below, are taken from Matthew 5:1-12 (NIV). We will examine them and see how they are signposts on the road to Christian maturity.

The Beatitudes

1. "Blessed are the poor in spirit, for theirs is the kingdom of heaven."

Entry into the kingdom of heaven comes through recognizing our spiritual poverty. Do we see ourselves as lacking what we need most in life beyond our physical needs? If we are self-sufficient, smug, and satisfied, we are a long way from the kingdom of heaven.

Consider the passage addressed to the church in Laodicea from the book of Revelation.

"To the angel of the church in Laodicea write:

> *"These are the words of the Amen, the faithful and true witness, the ruler of God's creation. I know your deeds, that you are neither cold nor hot. I wish you were either one or the other! So, because you are lukewarm—neither hot nor cold—I am about to spit you out of my mouth. You say, 'I am rich; I have acquired wealth and do not need a thing.' But you do not realize that you are wretched, pitiful, poor, blind and naked. I counsel you to buy from me gold refined in the fire, so you can become rich; and white clothes to wear, so you can cover your shameful nakedness; and salve to put on your eyes, so you can see.*
>
> *"Those whom I love I rebuke and discipline. So be earnest and repent. Here I am! I stand at the door and knock. If anyone hears my voice and opens the door, I will come in and eat with that person, and they with me."* (Revelation 3:14-20; NIV)

We must realize we are "poor, blind, and naked" – in need of the Savior before we are ready to enter God's Kingdom. So the first order of business in following Jesus is to recognize our spiritual poverty. Then we turn to Jesus, looking to Him in faith to provide what we lack.

2. "Blessed are those who mourn, for they will be comforted."

Once we realize our spiritual poverty and come to Jesus, trusting Him to provide what we lack, we are "born again." Then God gives us a new spiritual vision. As we look around and see the true condition of our world, we realize people who don't know Jesus are in a condition of wretchedness and extreme poverty and most may not even know it. Since we have been made aware of our own condition, we respond in compassion to their condition. We mourn over the spiritual poverty of mankind, knowing much is lacking in our lives. The Lord promises to comfort us and let us know He will work to deliver us and others out of our miserable condition.

3. "Blessed are the meek, for they will inherit the earth."

Meek is not *weak* but is actually a sign of quiet strength. Those who saw their own spiritual poverty came to Jesus and wept over their condition and the condition of the world. They had to go a step further. They had to realize, in their own strength, they were not able to create the changes they so earnestly desired and desperately needed. They had to first recognize they must fully rely on the Lord to accomplish the needed changes in them and in others through whatever means He chose. They believed the truth of Jesus's words, "... apart from Me, you can do nothing" (John 15:5b; ISV). They were also growing in faith and able to bear witness to another great truth that Jesus said, "... with God all things are possible" (Matthew 19:26b). They knew their strength to obey God must come from the Lord, realizing He is the Source to transform people and our world. Those who walk by faith will inherit the earth when it is transformed by the Lord.

4. "Blessed are those who hunger and thirst for righteousness, for they will be filled."

Those disciples who realize they are powerless to bring about the righteousness they need will also develop a hunger and thirst for it. They will desire more of the Lord because they know He alone is the source of the righteousness God requires. They will even have a deeper revelation: they will recognize the Lord Himself is our righteousness. They will hunger and thirst after knowing Him better and the Lord will satisfy them by drawing them into a more intimate relationship with Him.

5. "Blessed are the merciful, for they will be shown mercy."

Disciples, who know their poverty; come to Jesus; weep over the lack of righteousness in their world and in themselves; realize their inability to produce righteousness apart from Jesus, and earnestly seek after Jesus, will realize He is full of mercy. He does not administer justice to His disciples. Instead, He showers them with mercy. If not for His mercy, they would be undone by His holiness and righteousness which they could never obtain through their own efforts. As these disciples receive new mercies from God every morning, they show mercy to others they encounter in their daily walk. They are being transformed from those who judge others, demanding they measure up; to those who show mercy toward others, knowing no one can change without the Lord's help and power. These show themselves to be the Lord's disciples and will be recipients of His mercy in their present life on earth and in eternity. A passage following the Lord's Prayer shows the link between forgiveness and mercy:

> *"For if you forgive other people when they sin against you, your heavenly Father will also forgive you. But if you do not forgive others their sins, your Father will not forgive your sins."*
> (Matthew 6:14-15; NIV)

6. "Blessed are the pure in heart, for they will see God."

God's heart is absolutely pure and He continues to purify the hearts of His people. The disciples who have experienced and practiced God's mercy develop more of a heart like His. They grow in their hatred for sin and unrighteousness and learn to trust God to build holiness into their own lives. This holiness works itself out in practical ways such as walking righteously before men in the daily grind of life. God promises to reveal Himself to those who have purified their hearts through submitted to Him in reverential trust and worship. They will perceive God more clearly through the eyes of their hearts.

God uses various trials to refine our faith which He sees as more precious than gold. Those with purified hearts will be like Job who received this reward from the Lord after his terribly difficult trials. God will do for us what He did for Job through testing his faith and purifying his heart. After God revealed Himself to Job, Job said:

> *"My ears had heard of you but now my eyes have seen you. Therefore I despise myself and repent in dust and ashes."* (Job 42: 5-6; NIV)

As stanza five says in the famous classic hymn, *How Firm a Foundation, Ye Saints of the Lord*:

> "When through fiery trials thy pathway shall lie,
> My grace, all-sufficient, shall be thy supply.
> The flames shall not hurt thee; I only design,
> Thy dross to consume and thy gold to refine."

7. "Blessed are the peacemakers, for they will be called children of God."

After the disciple has gone through the necessary fiery trials for God to purify his heart, he is ready to join the Lord in His work. He can be trusted in the work of reconciling men to God and can be used to help bring it about. He is also qualified to help reconcile those who are in conflict with each other because he does not come as a judge but comes as one who has first cast the beam out of his own eye so he can see clearly to remove the mote from his brother's eye. He is now walking in the footsteps of Jesus as His brother and as a child of the same God Who is the Father of Jesus. People will see these disciples who walk in great peace as they follow the Prince of Peace and recognize it is only possible through God. They will be called the children of God by all those who are not blind. And as the Apostle John says,

> See what great love the Father has lavished on us, that we should be called children of God! And that is what we are! The reason the world does not know us is it did not know him. Dear friends, now we are children of God, and what we will be has not yet been made known. But we know that when Christ appears, we shall be like him, for we shall see him as he is. All who have this hope in him purify themselves, just as he is pure. (1 John 3:1-3; NIV)

8. "Blessed are those who are persecuted because of righteousness, for theirs is the kingdom of heaven."

Once the disciple is qualified through growing into Christ-likeness, God calls him into the ministry of reconciliation. He will be adding to God's kingdom and building up the body of Christ. God's enemies will become his enemies and he will be targeted because of his effectiveness in advancing God's kingdom. Satan will raise up those who will persecute him, not because of any wrong he has done but because he has done what is good in God's sight. God is using him to populate heaven and depopulate hell. The devil will try to shut this down. But God wants him to recognize he is blessed and what is happening to him is proof he is following in the footsteps of Jesus and doing what is well-pleasing to God. He is functioning in the kingdom of heaven because he is expanding it. His home is with Jesus and his effectiveness proves he is not of this world.

9. "Blessed are you when they revile and persecute you, and say all kinds of evil against you falsely for My sake. Rejoice and be exceedingly glad, for great is your reward in heaven, for so they persecuted the prophets who were before you."

The Ninth Beatitude personalizes and adds to the Eighth Beatitude. Note that Jesus says *when* not *if*. We will be persecuted, cursed, and lied about because of our stand for Christ. How are we to respond? Do we hit back hard against those who are reviling and persecuting us? Jesus would have us do the opposite of what is natural. He says we should bless those who persecute us and pray for those who despitefully use us. Now He says that we are to rejoice and be very glad that we are being persecuted for His sake! He says if we endure persecution because we are following Him, He will reward us greatly when He returns! We are following in the footsteps of the prophets. Now, that's something to think about!

The conditions of the hearts of these disciples fluctuate among the phases and conditions described in each of the Beatitudes. They can claim all of the blessings as they follow the Lord. They will continue to recognize their own poverty. They will continue to weep for the condition of the world and the lack of righteousness in the dark areas of their own hearts and lives. They will continue to recognize only Jesus can change them and others for the better. They will have a greater hunger for more of Him and they will receive a greater revelation of and deeper fellowship with Him. Their hearts will continue to be purified and they will grow in their ability to know and see God. They will walk in greater peace and be more reconciled to Jesus and to each other, proving they are the children of God. They will continue to be refined through persecution. It will go well with them in the end. The Lord will reward them with this commendation:

> *"His master replied, 'Well done, good and faithful servant! You have been faithful with a few things; I will put you in charge of many things. Come and share your master's happiness!'"* (Matthew 25:23; NIV)

Chapter 20 – Checking Your Progress through the Beatitudes

Pray, Study, Meditate, and Do

Key Scripture: *Now when Jesus saw the crowds, he went up on a mountainside and sat down. His disciples came to him, and he began to teach them.* (Matthew 5:1-2; NIV)

Ask God to help you as you work through this devotional study. Feel free to add to or change your answers at any time. You are encouraged to write all your answers.

1. During this week take some time to search your heart before God and discover where you are in your walk with the Lord with respect to following the progression shown in the Beatitudes.
2. Can you identify a time in your life when you felt you were "poor in spirit"? What happened to make you realize this?
3. Can you identify a time in your life when you grieved over your own spiritual condition and/or that of someone you loved and/or your culture? What motivated you to grieve? Be specific.
4. Can you identify a time in your life when you realized you didn't have the strength or resources to bring about the spiritual change you wanted for yourself? What did this realization motivate you to do, if anything?
5. Can you identify a time in your life where God awakened a hunger and thirst to know Him and to live a godly life? If you can remember, describe the conditions that brought this about. If the hunger and thirst didn't persist, do you remember what contributed to diminishing it? How do you think the hunger and thirst to know God and to live righteously can be renewed?
6. Consider these Bible passages. Identify and document qualities expressed in the Beatitudes through each passage. Consider how these qualities affected the person receiving them and how they affected the person practicing them. Write down your observations.

Acts 16:20-40 – Paul and the Philippian jailer

1 Samuel 24 – David's response when he had a chance to kill King Saul who had been pursuing him to kill him

Acts 7:57-60 – Stephen's response to those who were stoning him

Luke 23:33-48 – How Jesus died on the cross and how it affected others who watched

Genesis 18:16-21; 2 Peter 2:7-8–Lot's grieving over the conduct of those who lived in Sodom

1 Samuel 15:10 – 16:1–Samuel's grieving over King Saul's disobedience, resulting in the kingdom being eventually taken away from him

2 Kings 7:3-16–The starving lepers outside Jerusalem who found the camp of their enemies abandoned and their response

Acts 26–King Agrippa and Paul the apostle

Acts 8:1-8–What caused the early church in Jerusalem to be scattered

Luke 5:8–Peter asking the Lord to depart from him because he was a sinful man

Matthew 26:14–response to Jesus's kindness

Isaiah 6–Isaiah's response to his seeing a vision of the Lord

Matthew 14:13-21–The multitude who followed Jesus into the wilderness where He miraculously fed them

Exodus 3:1 – 4:17–Moses' response when God first sent him to Pharaoh

7. Use a concordance if necessary or an Internet search engine and find some other Bible passages describing qualities in the Beatitudes that relate to receiving God's blessing. Write down the references and identify the qualities and blessings identified in each passage.

Checking Your Progress through the Beatitudes

8. Ask God to help you find some Bible passages identifying a person reflecting a characteristic described in the Beatitudes and how that characteristic was used in their relationship with someone. Write the references down and identify the qualities. When the person exhibited the character trait described in the beatitude, what effect did it have on them and on the recipient of their action?

9. Do you remember a time in your life when you did something wrong that hurt someone and they extended mercy to you instead of judgment? How did it affect you? Do you remember a point in your life when you became predominantly merciful when wronged instead of demanding justice and judgment for those who hurt you? If you remember, how did this transformation occur? What are some of the results this transformation produced in your life?

10. What does it mean to have a pure heart? Where are you in the process of having your heart purified? How has your vision of God changed as you have progressed in this process? Who is responsible for purifying your heart? What is your part?

11. What does it mean to be a peacemaker? As a disciple of Jesus Christ, what do you think it means to be a peacemaker? What are some essential qualifications of a peacemaker? (Reflect on what you see in the lives of those you regard as peacemakers.) Who helped you make peace with God and what qualities did they show that helped you come to Christ? Where are you in the process of becoming a peacemaker?

12. Why do you think people are persecuted for doing what is right? Have you ever persecuted someone for doing what was right? If so, do you remember what motivated you to mistreat them because of what they did? Do you remember how they responded to you and how their response affected you? Have you ever been persecuted for doing the right thing? How did

you respond to suffering persecution from someone else? How did your response affect the person who mistreated you?

13. Choose one of the things God has shown you related to developing a characteristic expressed in the Beatitudes and work on making it into a habit and incorporating it into your life. Input it into your mobile device or write it on a 3" by 5" index card and carry it with you. Review it several times a day. See how you do and chart your progress.

Recommended resources and/or projects for those who want to go deeper: Read one of the Gospels and record instances where the various qualities expressed in the Beatitudes were reflected by Jesus or one of the Apostles. Were all of the qualities of the Beatitudes reflected by Jesus? Why or why not? If not, which quality or qualities did Jesus not reflect?

21

Your Pearl of Great Price

Love suffers long ... 1 Corinthians 13:4a

Jesus was the Master Teacher. He often conveyed spiritual truths through short stories or parables and explained their meaning to His disciples in private. One such parable was about a pearl of great price, the subject of this devotional study. In this parable, a merchant specializing in pearls searched everywhere to find the best pearls for his collection. One day he found a pearl unlike any other. Its size, shape, and texture were perfect and it was one of the largest he had ever seen, forming a perfectly round sphere with a flawless satin sheen.

He knew he just had to have that pearl! Of course, it was very expensive. But by selling all of his other pearls he realized he would have just enough money to purchase it. He did this gladly because he could see this pearl was one in a million. He had never seen a pearl so marked by its flawless beauty. It delighted him and captured his heart.

So where did this pearl come from and how was it made? Pearls are formed inside the oyster through a process. The oyster creates a pearl by protecting itself from an irritant it cannot get rid of such as a small grain of sand. The oyster keeps coating the irritant with a substance called mother of pearl. Over time, a pearl is formed. One could say the pearl is created as a result of and as a reaction to suffering brought on by an outside irritant that lives inside the oyster's shell.

Jesus finds the pearls He highly values in different places. He finds them in the hearts and character of his saints, especially those who have been patient in suffering through difficult trials, not of their own making. These are saints who endured their trials through love and commitment, refusing to take the easy way out by walking away. By the grace of God, they built up layer after layer of "mother of pearl" to insulate themselves against their painful experience and make the situation more bearable. Over time, a beautiful pearl had formed out of their response to suffering. Through God's provision of inner resources, something beautiful was created through the patient suffering and trials of His saints.

It is important to understand the pearl is not for the oyster that created it. The oyster was merely adapting to a difficult situation to minimize its suffering. The pearl and its value are for the oyster's master. So is it with us. The pearl created as a result of our suffering is not for us. It has great value to our Master. You see, Jesus has crafted the gates of the celestial city out of pearls – pearls of great price. The way of suffering opens the door for others to come into the Kingdom of God through you when you patiently endure your trials by the grace of God.

What is your pearl of great price? What has caused irritation and suffering that you couldn't get rid of? Are you availing yourself of the grace of God to construct a pearl of great price for your Master through your long trial? Perhaps your trial is through a committed relationship where your love is not returned and you are regularly rejected. Perhaps it is the bad temper of a spouse which consistently flares up and releases hurtful words that wound your heart. Perhaps it is a job you must keep that subjects you to hardship and gives you no sense of personal satisfaction or fulfillment. Do you trust the Master to control the intensity and duration of your trial?

Consider these words of the apostle Paul, how he responded to his suffering, and what God produced out of it.

> *And lest I should be exalted above measure by the abundance of the revelations, a thorn in the flesh was given to me, a messenger of Satan to buffet me, lest I be exalted above measure. Concerning this thing I pleaded with the Lord three times that it might depart from me. And He said to me, "My grace is sufficient for you, for My strength is made perfect in weakness." Therefore most gladly I will rather boast in my infirmities, that the power of Christ may rest upon me. Therefore I take pleasure in infirmities, in reproaches, in needs, in persecutions, in distresses, for Christ's sake. For when I am weak, then I am strong.* (2 Corinthians 12:7-10)

Is there something within you or your environment you cannot escape that has created much suffering for you? Will you yield to the Master and allow Him to fashion it into a pearl of great price and a doorway into His Kingdom for others to enter? Are you willing to avail yourself of the grace of God and trust Him to make something beautiful and lasting that can only come through the love that suffers long?

Chapter 21 – Your Pearl of Great Price

Pray, Study, Meditate, and Do

Key Scripture: *Love suffers long* ... 1 Corinthians 13:4a

Ask God to help you as you work through this devotional study. Feel free to add to or change your answers at any time. You are encouraged to write all your answers.

1. During this week take some time to search your heart before God to uncover situations where you have had to live with outside irritants that caused you significant suffering.
2. Can you identify a pearl formed in you from extended suffering, not of your own making? What were the pearl and the suffering you endured? How was the pearl formed through your suffering?
3. Can you identify a situation where something you did was a source of ongoing irritation in the life of a loved one, causing them suffering? Did you see a pearl forming in their life as a result of their ongoing suffering? What was the irritant and how did it cause them to suffer? What pearl was formed? How do you think it was formed?
4. Can you identify what happened to someone who walked away from ongoing suffering caused by someone else? When do you think it is best to walk away and when do you think it is best to seek the Lord for grace to endure?
5. Consider these Bible passages. Identify the sources of irritation, the suffering produced, how each person coped to endure, and what character qualities were formed as a result.

Book of Ruth – Naomi

Book of Ruth – Ruth

Genesis 39-40 – Joseph

Genesis 16, 17, 21 – Hagar

Daniel 1:8-20 – Daniel

Hebrews 10:34 – Recipients of the letter to the Hebrews

Hebrews 11 – Saints described in Hebrews 11

6. Use a concordance if necessary or an Internet search engine and find some other Bible passages where irritants from external trials produced suffering but eventually something of beauty and value was formed in the person who endured. Write down the references and identify the irritants, the resultant suffering, the response to the suffering, and the resultant beauty and value produced as identified in each passage.
7. Ask God to help you find Bible passages identifying what happens when people walk away prematurely from irritating circumstances rather than choosing to suffer and allowing God to produce something of value and beauty from their trial. Write down the references, the irritations, and the results.
8. Describe an irritating situation where you chose to walk away. Why did you walk away? What was the result? Do you have any regrets because of your choice?
9. Describe an irritating situation you chose to endure even though it caused extended suffering. Why did you stay in it? What was the result? Do you have any regrets?

10. Describe a situation where you irritated someone else and they chose to walk away. What was the result? Do you know whether they had any regrets because of their choice?
11. Choose one of the things God has shown you where an irritation has been causing you suffering and where you sense He wants you to endure instead of walking away. Seek Him for a strategy to cover the irritant with "mother of pearl," trusting Him to bring something of beauty and value to Him out of your patient endurance. Work on making your godly response into a habit and incorporating it into your life. Input it into your mobile device or write it on a 3" by 5" index card and carry it with you. Review it several times a day. See how you do and chart your progress.

Recommended resources and/or projects for those who want to go deeper: Read the Book of Job and see what he suffered and how God used his trial to bring something of great beauty and value to God out of his patient endurance. Write a short essay (about three pages) of your findings. Trace through the life of the Apostle Paul from the book of *Acts* and his letters in the New Testament, identifying sources of his suffering and the results from his patient endurance. Read the book of Daniel and trace through his challenges, noting his steadfastness, and seeing the results of his patient endurance.

22

YOUR VALLEY OF DRY BONES

He asked me, "Son of man, can these bones live?" I said, "Sovereign Lord, you alone know." Ezekiel 37:3 (NIV)

Most Christians are familiar with the prophecy in *Ezekiel* where he was given a vision of a valley of dry bones and its interpretation. Let's take a look.

> *The hand of the Lord was on me, and he brought me out by the Spirit of the Lord and set me in the middle of a valley; it was full of bones. He led me back and forth among them, and I saw a great many bones on the floor of the valley, bones that were very dry. He asked me, "Son of man, can these bones live?"*
>
> *I said, "Sovereign Lord, you alone know."*
>
> *Then he said to me, "Prophesy to these bones and say to them, 'Dry bones, hear the word of the Lord! This is what the Sovereign Lord says to these bones: I will make breath enter you, and you will come to life. I will attach tendons to you and*

make flesh come upon you and cover you with skin; I will put breath in you, and you will come to life. Then you will know that I am the LORD.'"

So I prophesied as I was commanded. And as I was prophesying, there was a noise, a rattling sound, and the bones came together, bone to bone. I looked, and tendons and flesh appeared on them and skin covered them, but there was no breath in them.

Then he said to me, "Prophesy to the breath; prophesy, son of man, and say to it, 'This is what the Sovereign LORD says: Come, breath, from the four winds and breathe into these slain, that they may live.'" So I prophesied as he commanded me, and breath entered them; they came to life and stood up on their feet—a vast army.

Then he said to me: "Son of man, these bones are the people of Israel. They say, 'Our bones are dried up and our hope is gone; we are cut off.' Therefore prophesy and say to them: 'This is what the Sovereign LORD says: My people, I am going to open your graves and bring you up from them; I will bring you back to the land of Israel. Then you, my people, will know that I am the LORD, when I open your graves and bring you up from them. I will put my Spirit in you and you will live, and I will settle you in your own land. Then you will know that I the LORD have spoken, and I have done it, declares the LORD.'" (Ezekiel 37:1-14; NIV)

The Lord spoke to me about this passage many times. It contains keys to the great revival the Lord wants to bring about in the Last Days before He returns. The key to this passage is in the way the Lord will bring about revival. He requires those He will use to learn the lessons found here.

First, the prophet was shown a vision. Then he was asked a question. "Can these dry bones live?" He understood there was no human way to know the answer. He responded correctly, "Sovereign Lord, You alone know." He could see the bones were very dry and, in the natural, there would be no way for them to come to life. Yet he knew the Lord was sovereign and with God all things are possible. This is the first lesson God's people must learn if God is going to use them to bring life to others. They cannot look only to the natural and process things through their natural minds. They must look to the Spirit and follow the walk of faith.

The second lesson for us to learn is to understand what made the bones get so dry. What made these people lose hope and abandon their confidence in God? What brought them back to life? The answer to both questions is whether they *continue to hear the Word of the Lord*. They heard circumstances. They heard human reasoning. And they heard human emotions and the opinions of man. But when they stopped hearing the Word of the Lord, they lost hope. When they started hearing the Word of the Lord again, their hope was being restored and they began to come back to life.

God's people will be required to go through their own dry bones experiences through their own valleys. They too will lose hope if they do not continue to hear the Word of the Lord. They must depend on the Spirit to breathe life into them to sustain them with daily manna even as the Israelites were sustained for forty years as they wandered through the wilderness. All of the original generation of those twenty years old and older died in the wilderness because they did not "hear the Word of the Lord." Only Joshua and Caleb entered the Promised Land because they had a different spirit and continued to believe God. The others often rejected God's Word and the leading of His Spirit. They were not walking by faith or believing the Spirit as He would speak to them through His servant, Moses.

This story was written to benefit and teach us. God's people must search for daily manna to sustain them through faith and hope as they go through their wilderness journey. They must be teachable. They must be willing to be led. They cannot rely on yesterday's manna. They must get daily guidance from the Lord to sustain them on their journey. "Man does not live by bread alone but by every word that comes from the mouth of God" (see Deut. 8:3, Matt. 4:4; ESV). They must feed on the Bread of Life on a daily basis. Jesus is the Manna that will sustain you and the Holy Bible is the place to search for Him.

Why is the wilderness experience necessary? God's people need to spend some time in the wilderness walking to and fro among the dry bones in order to understand what happened to the people who died there. They also must live by God's Word if the same fate is not going to overtake them. Their wilderness experience through their valley of dry bones is necessary to teach them compassion and to break all dependencies on anything but God and His Word for their lives. They must learn to rely only on God and what He provides. They must have hearts that prefer living in the wilderness with the Lord more than living in the Promised Land and experiencing all of its blessings without Him. The Lord must become their greatest love, towering over everything else.

Once they have come to this point, the people of God will know how to hear God and will be quick to obey Him. They will be able to share the life-giving Word of God — the Word God gave them to sustain them in their wilderness journey. They will not judge. They will not condemn. They will just speak life through the words God is giving them.

They will speak these words in a way that will convey the Nature of the One who gives His words to them. People will come to life as they hear these words. God will revive them. Hope will be restored. They will come together and become a mighty army ready to take part in the final battle that precedes the Lord's return.

Where are you in your personal wilderness journey? What are you learning that will help you speak life to the dry bones that come into your life? What has the Lord been speaking to you that produced life in you? Has God shifted you into a place of higher ministry yet?

If He is in the process of sifting you, He has a reason. Hear His Word and let it be life to you. Then He will shift you to the place He has for you to fulfill your destiny. He will use you to bring life to those dry bones where He directs you to speak. Just continue to hear the Word of the Lord and prophesy to the dry bones as He directs. Let all of your confidence be in Him and in Him alone, acknowledging He is the Sovereign Lord.

Chapter 22 – Your Valley of Dry Bones

Pray, Study, Meditate, and Do

Key Scripture: ***He asked me, "Son of man, can these bones live?" I said,***

"Sovereign Lord, you alone know." Ezekiel 37:3 (NIV)

Ask God to help you as you work through this devotional study. Feel free to add to or change your answers at any time. You are encouraged to write all your answers.

1. During this week take some time to search your heart before God and discover the location of your "valley of dry bones."
2. Can you identify a situation of extended trials and hardship where you began to lose hope? Describe the situation. What happened to your confidence in God? What was happening to your relationship with Him?
3. Can you identify a situation where you were about to lose hope but something happened just in time to rekindle your hope? Describe the situation and what happened. What was happening to your faith in God? Why?
4. Can you identify some situations where friends of yours have lost hope? Write them down. Did they abandon their faith in God? Why or why not?
5. Consider these Bible passages. Identify and write down the extended difficult circumstances of each character and if and how they responded to them without losing hope as expressed in each passage. Do you see how faith in God is tied to hope?

Genesis 37, 39:1 – 41:41 (Joseph)

1 Samuel 25: 2-42 (Abigail)

1 Samuel 18:10-30; 19 -31 (David)

Acts 23 – 26 (Paul)

Matthew 3: 1-15; 11: 2-15 (John the Baptist)

Revelation 1: 1-11 (the apostle John)

6. Use a concordance if necessary or an Internet search engine and find some other Bible passages portraying very difficult circumstances where the people were able to persevere and hold on to

hope and faith in God. Write down the references. Identify in each passage how those affected were able to hold on to hope and faith in God. Record how God used them to help others, if applicable.

7. Ask God to lead you to Bible passages identifying people going through very difficult circumstances, resulting in them losing hope or faith in God. Write the references down and the circumstances that resulted in a loss of hope or faith in God.

8. Do you know anyone who has gone through some very difficult circumstances and has not lost hope or faith in God, resulting in them becoming a better person? Describe the situation, what helped them survive without losing hope or faith in God, and how the experience made them a better person. Have they been able to help others because of what they went through? If so, how?

9. Can you identify some situations that were hope-killers or faith-killers in your life?

10. Can you identify some difficult situations you have gone through that would have been hope-killers for many but you held on to hope and your faith in God? What helped you survive? What benefit did holding on to hope and faith in God produce for you? Have you been better able to help others as a result? How? How do you think God valued your perseverance in maintaining your hope and faith in Him?

11. Choose the greatest hope-killer and/or faith-killer you are going through, have gone through, or might go through and ask God for a plan to help you or a loved one make it through such a trial without abandoning hope or faith in God. Work on "fleshing out" and implementing this plan for yourself by making it into a habit and incorporating it into your life. Input it into your mobile device or write it on a 3" by 5" index card and carry it with you. Review it several times a day. See how you do and chart your progress.

Recommended resources and/or projects for those who want to go deeper: Watch the movie, *Gettysburg*, or read a historically accurate book about the Civil War, such as *Best Little Stories from the Civil War* by C. Brian Kelly, and reflect on the trials the war brought and how the soldiers and citizens were able to cope. Write down some lessons you have learned through the characters in the film or the book you read about hope.

Read about the Apostle Paul in the book of Acts and the epistles he wrote and describe what you believe was his "valley of dry bones" and how he was able to walk through it without losing hope. Write a short essay (about three pages) and give references.

Read through the books of *Exodus*, *Numbers*, and *Deuteronomy* to get a sense of how the Lord sustained His people through their wilderness wanderings. Write a three-page essay about the highlights describing what stood out to you and why.

Destined to Reign with the King

Chapters 23-25

Anyone who has come this far and has established twenty or more character habits has made great progress in this course and is to be highly commended. You could not have succeeded without drawing closer to Jesus and learning to more fully surrender to Him and lean on His strength. He has been preparing you for a special place in His Kingdom. He is preparing you to reign with Him. The next three chapters explore what this means and help to prepare us for reigning with Him as we develop more of a Christian mindset and mature character.

Jesus is preparing His Bride to reign with Him as she walks by faith.

23

A BRIDE FOR THE KING

... Christ loved the church and gave Himself up for her to sanctify her, cleansing her by the washing with water through the word, and to present her to Himself as a glorious church, without stain or wrinkle or any such blemish, but holy and blameless. Ephesians 5:25b-27 (BSB)

She was absolutely stunning in her quietly-elegant ivory-and-white wedding gown skillfully intertwined with pearl and lace, her subdued but radiant face demurely hidden behind the matching white chiffon veil. There she was solemnly and deliberately slow-walking down the aisle in tune with the music of the *Wedding March*, momentarily stopping after each step. The tresses of her hair were held in place but seemed to flow together in a gentle stream of golden waves as she made her way to the altar in perfect poise. The bridesmaids had been escorted by the groomsmen, followed by the matron of honor escorted by the best man, and ending with the pastor and bridegroom walking down the aisle together. First, the bridesmaids, looking lovely in their handmade lace-accented teal dresses with taffeta sleeves, were each escorted by a groomsman in a complementary silver-grey tuxedo with matching teal bow tie and white carnation corsage. Next in the procession was the matron of honor escorted by the best man in similarly matched wedding attire. Finally, the pastor and I, both appropriately dressed, walked the aisle together as we made our way down to the front to join the rest of the wedding party in a balanced ceremony designed to honor men and women, bride and bridegroom.

But now all eyes were on the bride as I joined the others in patiently waiting at the altar. I suspect most hardly noticed her handsome escort, her brother Frank, in a smartly tailored tux who was there to give the bride away. She was lovely and I could hardly believe she would soon be mine, not just for a day but for the rest of our lives together! How good God is to bestow such gifts upon men! After all, He created the woman to complement the man and marriage was His idea from the beginning.

Have you ever wondered what a perfect bride would look like? She wouldn't be just beautiful to look at as was Uriah's wife, Bathsheba, during the time of King David. Without spot or blemish, her character and demeanor would be impeccable and beyond reproach. She would be a "perfect ten" and even more in every sense of the word; in body, soul, and spirit. We can be sure God's plan is to provide a perfect bride for His Son, the Lord Jesus Christ.

God has a plan to perfect the bride of Christ through His wisdom and power, through His Word, and by His Spirit. The details explaining how He'll do it are hidden in a mystery beyond our comprehension. The blood of Jesus Christ has washed away all of her sins while her imperfections are being removed through submission to the Word and Spirit of God. She will be cleansed from all idolatry and made worthy to be the bride for God's Beloved Son and will be clothed in the righteous deeds of the saints. She will be brought to maturity and perfected through the process God has designed. Even now she is busy making herself ready for her celestial wedding day.

Let's take a look at this process and gain insight into the character of God through considering some very special people of the Bible. We will consider Mary, the mother of Jesus, a woman of unparalleled faith and character. We will also consider Mary Magdalene, the first to see the risen Christ, with her unmatched devotion to Him. Jesus had been her life and His death left her completely undone. These women are worthy of careful study and the perfect bride will share their faith, devotion, and godly character.

We will also examine the genealogy of Jesus's mother, Mary (Luke 3: 23-38), and her husband, Joseph (Matthew 1: 1-16). We will consider Bathsheba and Solomon and contrast them with three unlikely people whom God used to do remarkable things: Rahab, Ruth, and Boaz. Rahab had been a prostitute and Ruth was a Moabite woman, both born of people who were enemies of God's people, the Israelites. Boaz followed his father in marrying a foreign woman from a people who were enemies of Israel that worshipped other gods. But that's only part of the story.

The most important part of the story is that all three had met their Redeemer and were people of faith whose previous identities had been transformed by God. God delights to make all things new! People like you and me are His specialty. So it doesn't matter what your past was or what your background has been. What matters is that you have met the Savior and He has been changing you, giving you a new and glorious identity in Him. Now, we'll return to the story.

As we examine the genealogies of Mary, Joseph, and Jesus we notice Boaz was an ancestor of all three. The Old Testament book of Ruth tells us how Boaz became the husband of Ruth, the Moabite woman. She was a widow and a daughter-in-law of Naomi but left her native land to embrace the people and, more importantly, the God of Naomi. Boaz's mother was Rahab, the harlot or prostitute. This is the Rahab who hid the two Israelite spies on the roof of her house in Jericho, the first city Israel was to conquer after wandering forty years in the desert and crossing the Jordan River. Boaz and Ruth would later have a grandson, David, who was destined to become the successor to Saul and the second king of Israel. David would later appoint Solomon as king, fulfilling his earlier promise to Bathsheba.

Now Solomon was King David's son. God greatly loved him and wanted David to name him *Jedediah* which means *loved by God*. Solomon started well by putting God first but later changed and ignored God's law by marrying many foreign women who worshiped other gods. In his old age, they turned his heart away from the Lord. Then Solomon was no longer fully devoted to the Lord as King David, his father had been. Perhaps King Solomon forgot that the Lord is a jealous God or he believed he was above God's law. Because of his compromised devotion to the Lord, ten of the twelve tribes of Israel would not be ruled by Solomon's descendants. For King David's sake, God left the remaining two tribes of Judah and Benjamin for David's and Solomon's descendants to rule.

Solomon's mother, Bathsheba, had been the wife of Uriah the Hittite. Uriah was one of an elite group of warriors who served King David with distinction. He was an honorable man with a noble character. His heart was with the army battling Israel's enemies. He refused to go home to his wife even after the King summoned him and made him drunk in an effort to hide Bathsheba's pregnancy that resulted from his adulterous affair. Instead, Uriah slept outside the palace. To cover his sin, David secretly ordered his general, Joab, to station Uriah in the most dangerous place of the battle where Israel's enemies would kill him.

Because Uriah was a man of standing in the kingdom of Israel as one of David's Mighty Men, Bathsheba had a life of prestige and status, living close to the king's palace. However, the biblical account reveals

Bathsheba was not a woman of faith and lacked discernment and godly character. She lacked discretion and bathed on a rooftop by the palace in the evening where a man could see her and desire her. She also did not resist King David's advances after he saw her bathing and lusted after her. She even consented to marry King David after he, unknown to her, had effectively murdered her husband to cover up the pregnancy from his adulterous affair. The baby they conceived in their adultery died. There is no biblical record of Bathsheba exercising faith in the Lord God of Israel. It appears her lack of faith in God, her unfaithfulness to her husband, and her poor character resulted in Bathsheba not being mentioned by name in the genealogical tables where she was referred to as "Uriah's wife."

Let's now return to Mary's husband, Joseph. His ancestry was traced through the line of kings ruling Israel, beginning with David and Solomon. It was sullied through unfaithful Bathsheba and idolatrous King Solomon. Even so, Joseph was a fine man of exceptional faith and character and was an excellent step-father to Jesus.

Jesus's human ancestry was through Mary, His mother, and included King David's son, Nathan. Neither Bathsheba nor King Solomon was included in Mary's or Jesus's lineage. But Boaz, Rahab, and Ruth were ancestors of both Joseph and Mary, his wife. Let's take a closer look at these three, beginning with Rahab.

God's amazing grace is revealed through His choosing Rahab as a descendant of His Son, Jesus, even though she had been a harlot or prostitute who lived among the enemies of Israel. What mattered most to God was that she was a woman of faith in the God of Israel and put her life on the line to hide the two Israelite spies. Because of this act of courage, her household was the only one spared when Jericho was attacked and its walls collapsed.

Rahab followed the instruction of the two spies and hung a scarlet ribbon from her window so she and those in her house would be spared. The scarlet ribbon was a biblical *type* and pointed to the blood of Jesus which shields us from God's wrath through our faith in Him. It was like the blood of the Passover lamb applied to the doorposts of the children of Israel. When the death angel saw it, he would pass over their houses and spare their firstborn sons. It was also like the time Abraham prepared to sacrifice his son, Isaac, at God's command but was told to sacrifice the ram God provided instead. These types pointed to the sacrifice God had in mind that would be used to spare us and our children from the consequences of our sins. Each of these examples pointed to Jesus Christ, the Lamb of God, Who takes away the sin of the world.

Now we'll take a closer look at Ruth and Boaz. As a Moabite woman, Ruth was excluded from participating in God's covenant with Israel whereas Boaz was the son of a prostitute whose mother was a foreigner. Yet both Ruth and Boaz were people of exceptionally fine character, accepting and honoring the Lord as their God. Boaz's mother and father had raised him well. And Naomi was like a mother to Ruth, drawing her to Naomi's God Whom she embraced as her own.

God honored Ruth and gave her Boaz as a husband. Ruth was chosen as part of the lineage of our Lord Jesus Christ. Ruth loved Naomi and entrusted her future to the hands of Naomi and the God of Israel. God honored her faith and her love and accepted her into His family and the family line of Jesus Christ even though her natural lineage as a Moabite would have excluded her from Israel.

Moabites were excluded from Israel partly because one of their kings, Balak, had tried to entrap Israel into sin to bring God's curse down upon them. Previously Balak had tried to hire a prophet of God to curse the Israelites because they were a threat to his people. This fascinating story includes a talking donkey and is recorded in Numbers, chapters 22-24. It shows outside forces are powerless to stop God from blessing His people.

The Moabites descended from Moab who was conceived through an act of deception and drunken incest, planned by his mother and perpetrated against his grandfather, Lot. Lot, Abraham's nephew, knew God but put material prosperity above spiritual prosperity when he chose to live in Sodom. He lost everything including his family. His daughters were immoral and not women of faith. Their names are not recorded in Scripture as part of the ancestral line. They ignored God's will and resorted to the arm of the flesh to try to accomplish their own will.

These genealogies and biblical records show what matters to God is not our past but our future. He requires us to turn from trusting in ourselves to trusting in His Son, Jesus, to receive life from Him. This takes faith. He is willing to give us the faith if we are willing to receive it. God opened the door for a descendant of Moab to become a great grandmother to King David and for a harlot or prostitute to become a great-great-grandmother to King David. Both Rahab and Ruth were part of the family line of Jesus Christ, cleansed through faith in believing God and acting on what they believed.

See how great our God is! Don't despair about your past! Turn your eyes to Jesus and believe His promises. Embrace Him and the new life He has to offer. God will gladly receive you into His Kingdom. The invitation is for all who are willing to turn from their self-trust and put their faith and trust in God and His Word.

The key to our transformation is in our focus. As we behold our King, we become like Him. The bride of Christ will be a perfect image of the Lord of Glory. When He comes, she will be ready and she will be like Him. Even now she is making herself ready. Consider these scriptures and be ready!

Beloved, now are we the sons of God, and it doth not yet appear what we shall be: but we know that, when he shall appear, we shall be like him; for we shall see him as he is.
1 John 3:2 (KJV)

Now we see things imperfectly, like puzzling reflections in a mirror, but then we will see everything with perfect clarity. All I know now is partial and incomplete, but then I will know everything completely, just as God now knows me completely.
1 Corinthians 13:12 (NLT)

And we, who with unveiled faces all reflect the glory of the Lord, are being transformed into His image with intensifying glory, which comes from the Lord, who is the Spirit.
2 Corinthians 3:18 (BSB)

Chapter 23 – A Bride for the King

Pray, Study, Meditate, and Do

Key Scripture: *... Christ loved the church and gave Himself up for her to sanctify her, cleansing her by the washing with water through the word, and to present her to Himself as a glorious church, without stain or wrinkle or any such blemish, but holy and blameless.*
Ephesians 5:25b-27 (BSB)

Ask God to help you as you work through this devotional study. Feel free to add to or change your answers at any time. You are encouraged to write all your answers.

1. During this week take some time to search your heart before God and discover where you are in your journey with God and where you see yourself in the process of becoming a member of the perfect bride, the Bride of Christ.
2. Do you remember what led you to first put your faith in Jesus Christ as Savior? Write your memories down.
3. Can you remember other times in your life when you have consistently shown faith in Jesus Christ as Lord? Write them down.
4. Can you identify some wrinkles or blemishes God has removed from your character since you became a Christian? How did He remove them? Describe the process.
5. Consider these Bible passages. Identify and write down positive or negative characteristics of one or more of God's people (usually but not always Israel or the Church) as expressed in each passage.

   Genesis 3:1-6

   Genesis 22:1-12

   Genesis 6:5-22

   Genesis 39:7-10

   2 Samuel 11

   Acts 5:1-11

   Acts 8:9-24

Acts 9:10-19

Luke 1:26-38

6. Use a concordance if necessary or an Internet search engine and find some other Bible passages describing characteristics of the bride of Christ. Write down the references and identify what characteristics they identify.
7. Ask God to lead you to find some Bible passages identifying flaws in God's people (Israel or the Church). Write the references down and the people and flaws they point to.
8. Are you aware of any current wrinkles or blemishes in your character you believe God wants to remove? What are they?
9. Ask God to show you a few areas of your character where He has worked with you to improve since you became a Christian. Document what process He used to help you improve in these areas of character development.
10. Ask God to show you a few areas of your character where you can improve with God's help and ask Him for some ideas on how you can develop a better character in these areas. Write these things down.
11. Choose a character quality God wants you to more fully develop and seek His plan and leadership to help you incorporate it into your life as a habit. Input it into your mobile device or write it on a 3" by 5" index card and carry it with you. Review it several times a day. See how you do and chart your progress.

Recommended resources and/or projects for those who want to go deeper: Read the *Song of Songs (Song of Solomon)* and focus on the characteristics of the Shulamite woman who was to be Solomon's bride. Write down a description of her and of her character qualities.

24

RULING WITH JESUS

Here is a trustworthy saying: If we died with him, we will also live with him; if we endure, we will also reign with him. If we disown him, he will also disown us; if we are faithless, he remains faithful, for he cannot disown himself.
2 Timothy 2: 11-13 (NIV)

This devotional study is about how we can prepare to rule with Jesus. To understand how this is to be done we will trace through key passages of the Bible to see why God created man and what He expects of man when it comes to ruling. We begin in the first chapter of Genesis where God created man and woman and gave them the authority to have dominion and rule over the earth.

> *Then God said, "Let Us make man in Our image, according to Our likeness; let them have dominion over the fish of the sea, over the birds of the air, and over the cattle, over all the earth and over every creeping thing that creeps on the earth." So God created man in His own image; in the image of God He created him; male and female He created them. Then God*

> *blessed them, and God said to them, "Be fruitful and multiply; fill the earth and subdue it; have dominion over the fish of the sea, over the birds of the air, and over every living thing that moves on the earth." (Genesis 1: 26-28, NKJV)*

After the fall of man and as a result of the curse, Adam would rule over Eve.

> *To the woman He said: "I will greatly multiply your sorrow and your conception. In pain you shall bring forth children. Your desire shall be for your husband, and he shall rule over you." (Genesis 3:16)*

As we study the Bible, we see God's original intention was not for people to rule over other people. His Word was to rule over them. He appointed men like Moses to teach them His Word and Joshua to lead them into the Promised Land. God chose men who simply followed His instructions. As the people obeyed God's Word, they had no visible king and needed none because God was their King.

> *So Moses came and told the people all the words of the LORD and all the judgments. And all the people answered with one voice and said, "All the words which the LORD has said we will do." And Moses wrote all the words of the LORD. . . . Then the LORD said to Moses, "Come up to Me on the mountain and be there; and I will give you tablets of stone, and the law and commandments which I have written, you may teach them." (Exodus 24: 3-4a, 12)*

After the time of Moses and Joshua, the Lord spoke to His people through the angel of the Lord to give them direction and instruction even when they rebelled against the Lord (see Judges 1:2; 2:1-20). The people turned away from the Lord after Joshua and the elders of Israel died. Then God appointed judges to lead the people to obey Him and

His Word. The Lord was with the judges but, when they died, Israel turned away from the Lord time and again as recorded in the book of Judges.

Israel's last judge was Samuel who was also a prophet and functioned as a priest. Samuel faithfully obeyed the Lord and taught the people to do what was right. Toward the end of his life, his sons were made priests in his stead. However, they did not follow in his steps but perverted justice and Israel rebelled. Israel wanted to be like the other nations and rejected the Lord as their king. God finally gave them a king but subjected him to restrictions. The only king who was to rule over them with complete authority was the Lord Jesus Christ who would come many years later.

To sum it up, God spoke through His prophets to offer correction and instruction. He installed priests to accept the sacrifices He required in the manner He prescribed. When the priests stopped doing what God required, the people rebelled and asked for a king.

God, the Father, has given all authority in heaven and on earth to the Lord Jesus Christ. He is the King of kings and Lord of lords. He shall rule the nations with a rod of iron. When He has put down all His adversaries, He will hand over everything to His Father, God. ("Then the end will come, when he hands over the kingdom to God the Father after he has destroyed all dominion, authority and power." (1 Corinthians 15:24; NIV)

Christians who endure or share in the first resurrection shall reign with Jesus (2 Timothy 2:12; Revelation 20:6). He will reward the faithful with more responsibility to rule (Luke 19:17) and will give great authority to those who overcome and continue to do His will to the end (Revelation 2:26-27). The Lord will be united and rule with His Bride (the Church) during the millennial period (see Revelation 20:1-6).

God's sons and daughters will be one with Him. It will be one big happy family and there will be no need for earthly kings. Jesus Christ and God, the Father will reign forever.

The Lord's Prayer also shows God is the One who rules. "Thy kingdom come. Thy will be done on earth as it is in heaven. ... For Thine is the kingdom and the power and the glory forever and ever." So God will reign over everything for all of eternity. But it will be a joyous harmony as His people gladly obey Him. The Bride of Christ will join Him in ruling over the new creation and God will rule over all of His sons and daughters.

Father God and the Lord Jesus Christ will joyfully rule over all of His people when His eternal kingdom has become the kingdom of this world. There will be only one throne, the throne of God and of the Lamb. In the meantime, the Church is seated with Christ in the heavenly places at the right hand of God the Father. We are seated with Him on His throne and we reign with Him over all He gives us until His eternal kingdom is completely established. In Christ, we have authority over principalities and powers and nature but not over each other. God the Father rules us through the Lord Jesus Christ.

> *And he showed me a pure river of water of life, clear as crystal, proceeding from the throne of God and of the Lamb. In the middle of its street, and on either side of the river, was the tree of life, which bore twelve fruits, each tree yielding its fruit every month. The leaves of the tree were for the healing of the nations. And there shall be no more curse, but the throne of God and of the Lamb shall be in it, and His servants shall serve Him.* (Revelation 22:1-3)

Ruling with Jesus will be glorious and we should practice doing it now. We must first be ruled by the Word of God and subject to Jesus in obedient trust. Being ruled by Jesus and God the Father is even more glorious and shall be our eternal state. No more sin. No more pain. No more death. No more separation. Just a joyful oneness with the Father, the Son, and the Holy Spirit! What a glorious and eternal day that will be!

Chapter 24 – Ruling with Jesus

Pray, Study, Meditate, and Do

Key Scripture: *Here is a trustworthy saying: If we died with him, we will also live with him; if we endure, we will also reign with him. If we disown him, he will also disown us; if we are faithless, he remains faithful, for he cannot disown himself.* 2 Timothy 2: 11-13 (NIV)

Ask God to help you as you work through this devotional study. Feel free to add to or change your answers at any time. You are encouraged to write all your answers.

1. During this week take some time to search your heart before God and discover where you are in the process of dying, living, enduring, and reigning with Jesus.
2. Can you identify a particular time where you made a decision to die with Jesus? What triggered that decision and how did it work out for you?
3. Can you identify a particular time where you have experienced living with Jesus? How did that come about and how did it work out for you?

4. Can you identify a season of life where you have had to endure because of your walk with Jesus? Describe it and how it worked out for you.
5. Consider these Bible passages. Identify and write down how God's people are exercising His authority as expressed in each passage.

    Exodus 3:1-12

    Matthew 14:3-12

    Genesis 2:19-20

    Genesis 39:2-12, 20-23; 40:8; 41:9-44

    Genesis 6:8-22

    Acts 13:2-5; 14:21-28; Galatians 1:1-2; 2:7-9

    Hosea, chapters 1 and 3

6. Use a concordance if necessary or an Internet search engine and find some other Bible passages about reigning with Christ. Write down the references and identify the areas of authority they identify.
7. Ask the Lord to lead you to some Bible passages identifying people who were enabled to exercise God's authority because they were under His authority. Write the references down and the areas of authority identified in each passage. Include identifying who exercised God's authority and how they did it.
8. Has there been a season in your life where you believe you have been reigning with Jesus? Describe this season and why

you believe you were reigning with Him. How did it work out for you?

9. Have you ever been tempted to turn your back on Jesus or deny Him? What were the circumstances and the condition of your heart contributing to this temptation? How did turn out for you? If you yielded to the temptation, what brought you back to Jesus?

10. What does it mean to disown Jesus? Have you ever felt like disowning Him? What kept you from it?

11. Do you know anyone who seemed to walk with Jesus in the past but later seemed to have disowned Him? Do you know what happened to cause them to turn their back on Jesus and walk away from Him? Do you think you could be tempted similarly? How can you strengthen yourself to prevent this from happening?

12. Ask God to show you a few things hindering you from walking in your full authority with Him. Ask Him to show you any areas where you are not fully under His authority.

13. Choose an area God has identified for you to submit more completely to Him and seek His help in habitually submitting to His authority in this area so you can more completely exercise His authority. Input it into your mobile device or write it on a 3" by 5" index card and carry it with you. Review it several times a day. See how you do and chart your progress.

Recommended resources and/or projects for those who want to go deeper: Do a character study of Moses from Exodus to Deuteronomy to see how he came under God's authority and exercised it. Make note of his failures and their consequences as well. Write a three-page report about what you learned and include examples.

25

Conclusion: He Is Worth It and so Are You!

For God so loved the world, that he gave his only begotten Son, that whosoever believeth in him should not perish, but have everlasting life. John 3:16 (KJV)

How much is a soul worth? How much do you value your soul? How much is *your* soul worth? God decides the value of His creation, not us. But how do we value ourselves and others? This is the subject of this devotional study.

God sees our most valuable possession as our soul. He says it is worth more than the combined wealth of the whole world. He also puts a premium on the value of His own children. These facts should put things into perspective for us as we consider what we value.

Jesus said, "And what do you benefit if you gain the whole world but lose your own soul? Is anything worth more than your soul?" (Mark 8:36-37; NLT)

Conclusion: He Is Worth It and So Are You!

"Since you are precious and honored in my sight, and because I love you, I will give people in exchange for you, nations in exchange for your life." (Isaiah 43:4; NIV)

God made man as the crowning glory of His creation, in His image and likeness. He gave man the authority to rule the world He created. But God intended to rule man through His Word, by His Spirit, and through His Son. God also instituted the death penalty for any person or animal who murdered a human being. It was an attack against God which resulted in the forfeiture of the life of the attacker. God gave this prohibition to protect human life because He loves us and values us above the rest of His natural creation.

We were made to love and to be loved. It is our highest priority to love God first. Then we are to love our neighbor as ourselves. What does this mean? Among other things, it means we must love and value ourselves. We cannot love and value others properly if we do not first love ourselves in a healthy way. We are to love God first and foremost with all that we are. Then we are to love those made in His image and likeness even though they have been tragically marred by sin.

God values us so highly that He sent His only begotten Son to die for us. God values us as highly as He values Himself. Yet He honors our choice. It is up to us to choose whether we will have Him rule over us or not. Christians have chosen to submit to God's rule through His Son, the Lord Jesus Christ. We do not do it perfectly and we continue to make progress slowly but we acknowledge Jesus Christ is Lord.

God also values His people above those who steadfastly worship idols. Yet he values the lost enough to have sent His Son to die for them. Even today Christians are still being martyred for the sake of reaching the lost. Jesus promised that those who follow Him will be rewarded. It may cost us everything to be a disciple of Jesus Christ but, even in this world, we will receive a lot more than we give up, and we will receive eternal life in the world to come.

Jesus laid down His life for the sake of His Bride, the Church. He cherishes her. Father God gave the life of His only begotten Son for the sake of having other sons and daughters. He cherishes them as He cherishes His only begotten Son. God calls us into oneness with Himself – with the Father, with the Son, and with the Holy Spirit. It is a holy calling beyond description and it cost God His unspeakable gift to make it possible and a reality for those who respond to His call. We are worth it in God's sight!

The book of Revelation identifies Jesus as the only One in heaven or on earth Who is worthy to open up the scrolls. He is the priceless and matchless Son of God and God the Son. His love is beyond comprehension or description. He poured Himself out freely for us because of this great love for us. When we receive Him we receive His love.

God is all about love and His love is directed toward us. God restores His image and likeness in us through the working of His Holy Spirit. The Holy Spirit provides the power to transform us into people that love. Father God actively fathers us to help us grow to maturity. The Lord Jesus leads by example. He tells us what to do and shows us how. Jesus is the perfect bridegroom and He is worthy of the perfect bride, His church. Jesus showed us the greatest love anyone could give when He laid down His life for us.

The perfect Father loved us so dearly He sacrificed His Son for us so we might have life with Him. When we turn to Him, He welcomes us like prodigal sons and daughters coming home. He is Love and He is worth our following and submitting to Him. We belong to Him and He wants us to willingly submit to His will and commands which are always given with our best interests in mind.

Conclusion: He Is Worth It and so Are You!

> *What? Know ye not your body is the temple of the Holy Ghost which is in you, which ye have of God, and ye are not your own? For ye are bought with a price: therefore glorify God in your body, and in your spirit, which are God's.* (1 Corinthians 6:19-20; KJV)

It was God's will for Jesus to die for us. He purchased us with His precious blood because we are precious in His sight, and honored, and He loves us (Isaiah 43:4). The bride is worthy of the bridegroom and the bridegroom is worthy of the bride. Jesus is not ashamed to call us brothers and acknowledge we are sons and daughters of God. God is not ashamed to receive us as His children in spite of all our failings and shortcomings which He no longer sees. He will purify us and make us completely holy. All sin will be forever removed from us and we will have the perfect righteousness of Christ. God has willed this and will accomplish it through His Holy Spirit and Word, and through the blood and name of our Lord Jesus Christ.

Only in this life can you yield to God and allow Him to use you to build His eternal kingdom. His life must replace our own for His will to be done in and through us.

> *"I have been crucified with Christ, and I no longer live, but Christ lives in me. The life I live in the body, I live by faith in the Son of God, who loved me and gave Himself up for me."* (Galatians 2:20; BSB)

Following Jesus is worth it and so are you!

Chapter 25 – Conclusion: He Is Worth It and So Are You!

Pray, Study, Meditate, and Do

Key Scripture: *For God so loved the world, that he gave his only begotten Son, that whosoever believeth in him should not perish, but have everlasting life.* John 3:16 (KJV)

Ask God to help you as you work through this devotional study. Feel free to add to or change your answers at any time. You are encouraged to write all your answers.

1. During this week take some time to search your heart before God and discover how much you value Jesus Christ and how much you value yourself.
2. Can you identify what basis you have for valuing yourself?
3. Can you identify what basis God has for valuing you?
4. Can you identify what basis you have for valuing others?
5. Can you identify what basis you have for valuing Jesus Christ?
6. Can you identify what basis you have for valuing God, the Father?
7. Can you identify what basis you have for valuing the Holy Spirit?
8. Consider these Bible passages. Identify and write down the basis for valuing the person or persons as expressed in each passage.

John 3:16

Romans 5:6-8

Conclusion: He Is Worth It and so Are You!

Isaiah 43:4

Acts 4:8-12

Matthew 22:34-40

9. Use a concordance if necessary or an Internet search engine and find some other Bible passages showing how much God values people and why He values them so highly. Write down the references and identify the basis God uses to value people as identified in each passage.
10. Ask God to lead you to some Bible passages identifying how much Jesus Christ is valued by God, the Father, and by others. Write the references down and the basis each reference gives for valuing Jesus Christ.
11. What are the top two or three things you value in a person? Why do you value these things? Why are they at the top of your list?
12. What do you think are among the top two or three things God values in a person? Why do you think He values those things and why are they at the top of His list? Support your answers with Scripture.
13. What are the top two or three things you value about Jesus Christ and why are they at the top of your list?
14. What are the top two or three things you value about God, the Father, and why are they at the top of your list?
15. What are the top two or three things you value about the Holy Spirit and why are they at the top of your list?
16. Ask God to show you a few things you value very highly and ask Him to help you realign your heart by highly valuing what He highly values. Write down the values He would like to put into your heart and the values in your heart He wants to replace with higher values.

17. Choose a quality God has shown you He highly values and ask Him to help you realign your heart to better reflect this quality. Work on incorporating making this quality habitually highly valued in your life. Input it into your mobile device or write it on a 3" by 5" index card and carry it with you. Review it several times a day. See how you do and chart your progress.

Recommended resources and/or projects for those who want to go deeper: Write a love letter to a loved one (spouse, child, parent, sibling, other) and tell them how much you value them. Give them specific instances of how they have expressed the qualities that you highly value. The letter should be a type-written page or two in length although you may want to write it in longhand. Be sure to sign it. Frame the letter and present it to your loved one as a gift. You may want to do this for several loved ones and present it to them on their birthday, your anniversary, or some other special day.

Looking Back and Moving Forward
Chapter 26

To have reached this point and successfully developed twenty-four new character habits is worthy of a gold medal! Of course, you will have to share it with Jesus or just give it to Him because He is the One Who has brought you this far! He will share His throne with you so I am sure He will share this medal with you too! After you finish this course by completing the next chapter and nailing down your last two habits, I would like to hear from you.

You may contact me through my publisher and through the contact information provided in this book. I would like to know how God has used this course to help you become more like Jesus. Some of those who contact me after successfully completing this course may be asked to write a recommendation to encourage others to take this or my next course. If your recommendation is used I will give you a signed copy of this book and the next book as a way of saying "thank you"!

Be blessed! You're the best!

We can look back to where we were and with excited anticipation, look forward to where we are going!

26

Rejoicing in your Progress and Suggestions For Moving Forward

For whatever is born of God overcomes the world. And this is the victory that has overcome the world—our faith. Who is he who overcomes the world, but he who believes Jesus is the Son of God? 1 John 5:4-5

Congratulations! After completing this devotional study you will have successfully completed *A Disciple's Journey, Volume 1*. You may have found some of the devotionals challenging and several of the *Pray, Study, Meditate, and Do* portions even more challenging. Even if you have a personal coach to assist you in an exercise program, you may not successfully complete all parts of the program in your early attempts. A good coach doesn't do his job if the exercises he assigns are too easy or if they do not help you to reach your long-term goals. If you have ever been on a diet you also know that sometimes you get "off the wagon." But that's no reason to give up and drop out! If you had someone to hold you accountable for dieting or for an exercise program, they would tell you to just hit the "reset" button and get back on track to move forward. The same thing applies to this course and your walk as a disciple of Jesus Christ.

You may find it helpful to write down the things or events that got you off track and find a way to successfully overcome them the next time. You will also discover developing godly habits will help you overcome inertia and negative feelings such as discouragement. Designating a time and a place for your devotional "diet" will help you develop the habit. Putting into practice what you learn from your devotional studies will help you to grow as a Christian. This takes a plan and a purpose.

I first developed a daily-quiet-time habit with God many years ago through a weekly discipleship group led by my senior pastor and designed to establish the habit of spending an hour a day with God. We met weekly and were held accountable and encouraged as we reported our successes and failures each week. We would get prayer support, encouragement, and godly wisdom from the group and the pastor. He believed developing a consistent daily devotional time was foundational for a growing Christian to mature. His goal was for each of us to establish the habit of spending an hour a day alone with God in prayer, Bible study, and meditation.

If we establish a regular devotional time with God it will serve as a bulwark against the onslaught of sinful temptations including materialism, secularism, and other false ideologies. I have been most successful in doing daily devotionals when I made them a high priority. Establishing a regular devotional time with God is not an end but it is a beginning. Connecting to God and having a life that flows with His life is a 24-7 process when it is at the level of maturity Jesus demonstrated.

I believe you can incorporate a devotional study into your daily time with God by spending an average of thirty minutes or so a day to pray,

Rejoicing in Your Progress

read, study, meditate, and do what is indicated. Avoid trying to do the devotional studies as a work of the flesh where you are depending on your own ability to discipline yourself. It should take you around a year to incorporate twenty-six new or improved character habits to help you mature as a Christian. You must depend on the Lord and His direction to succeed as a disciple who is drawing closer to Jesus.

Each devotional study should be a springboard for one new habit which I am trusting the Holy Spirit to reveal to you as you seek Him about it. If the Holy Spirit doesn't show you something He wants you to work on, just go to the next devotional study. If He shows you several things to work on from one devotional, follow His lead. This course is intended to be only a guideline to help you in your Christian walk. The Holy Spirit is the One you must learn to follow closely if you are going to go on to Christian maturity. You can always return to the devotional studies at a later time. You do not even need to follow the order of the book in doing the devotional studies even though this might be the best way because later devotional studies often build on earlier ones. You may also want to review a previous devotional study before going on to the next one.

Jesus said, "Man does not live by bread alone but by every word that proceeds out of the mouth of God." This means everything God put in the Bible is there to help us. If we only read the New Testament or exclude other parts of the Bible, we are restricting our spiritual diet and will be eliminating some necessary spiritual nutrients. As a result, our spiritual growth will be hindered. The Bible promises success to those who meditate on God's Word day and night. (See Joshua 1 and Psalm 1.) Other passages instruct us to put what we read into practice. "But be ye doers of the word, and not hearers only, deceiving your own selves." (James 1:22; KJV)

I would encourage you to set some goals for yourself such as to read the Bible through in a year and/or to read a daily devotional such as Oswald

Chamber's, *My Utmost for His Highest*. I have found these goals helpful in the past and have continued doing them for many years. I have chosen different translations of the Bible for some of those years as each translation can give a fresh perspective and enrich your understanding.

Cultivating an appetite for God and His Word is vital but sometimes our experiences in life can take that appetite away. When we eat too much spiritual junk food it takes away our appetite for good nutritious spiritual food. When we spend too much time in worldly endeavors it affects our thinking and dulls our spirits. We become spiritually weak and unhealthy. The Bible says if we love the world the love of the Father is not in us (see 1 John 2:15).

Chapter 26 – Rejoicing in your Progress and Suggestions for Moving Forward

Pray, Study, Meditate, and Do

Key Scripture: *For whatever is born of God overcomes the world. And this is the victory that has overcome the world—our faith. Who is he who overcomes the world, but he who believes Jesus is the Son of God?* 1 John 5:4-5

Ask God to help you as you work through this devotional study. Feel free to add to or change your answers at any time. You are encouraged to write all your answers.

1. During this week take some time to seek the Lord for His plan to strengthen your faith and help you move forward as a

Christian. It may include reading a devotional and having a plan to read through the Bible or the New Testament in a year.

2. Wise Christians recommend choosing a specific time and place to meet with God each day to get to know Him better. Can you identify an interruption-free time each day when you can meet with God for prayer, Bible study, and meditation? Some have found early morning while other household members are still sleeping works well. It may not be the same time each day based on your schedule. When would you like to meet with the Lord?

3. It is good to choose a place where distractions such as phone calls and other interruptions can be kept to a minimum. Ask the Lord to show you a specific place where you can meet with Him for your daily quiet time. Sometimes the place may change based on your schedule and location. Where would you like to meet with the Lord?

4. At a minimum, you should have a Bible and a concordance or computer with ready access to the Internet or electronic Bible as well as a pen and a pad or a word-processing program on your computer. You may want to write down what God shows you. Include prayer requests as well as answers to prayer. Can you identify specific resources you will use for your daily meeting with God? Make a plan with a starting date and assemble all of the materials you will need. It may help to join a small group of like-minded people or to have a Christian friend join you in making this commitment so you can support each other and hold each other accountable. Write down your plan and your start date. Then "just do it!" The main thing is to get up and go on even if you fail more than a few times. Keep at it until the devotional habit is firmly established. Then it will be easier to maintain.

5. Consider these Bible passages. Identify and write down the main Bible character or characters and devotional habits demonstrated as expressed in each passage.

Daniel 1:8-21

Daniel 6

Joshua 1:1-10

James 1:22; 2:14-26

Genesis 5:21-24

Acts 10:1–11:18

John 4:1-42

6. Use a concordance if necessary or an Internet search engine and find some other Bible passages showing devotional habits developed by godly people. Write down the references and identify the devotional habit(s) they identify.
7. Ask God to lead you to some Bible passages identifying things that caused those who walked with God to stumble and to turn away from God. Record the references, the character, and the causes of stumbling revealed in each passage.
8. What has caused you to stumble in your walk with God in the past?
9. What is your greatest current struggle or what has been your greatest recent struggle in maintaining a growing and intimate walk with God?
10. Ask God to show a few things you can do to keep on track in developing a growing relationship with Him. Record what He shows you.
11. Choose one of the things God has shown you that will enhance your walk with Him and work on making it into a habit and incorporating it into your life. Input it into your mobile device

or write it on a 3" by 5" index card and carry it with you. Review it several times a day. See how you do and chart your progress.

Recommended resources and/or projects for those who want to go deeper: Do a character study on the life of Abraham, Moses, David, Paul, or Jesus, taking special note of their devotional habits. You can choose any of the prophets or any of the apostles if you wish. Watch the movie, *War Room*, by Sherwood Pictures. It may help strengthen your resolve and help you develop an effective daily quiet time.

TO BE CONTINUED ... If you enjoyed going through Volume 1, be looking for *A Disciple's Journey, Volume 2* which should be coming out next year. Please check my Web page for special offers.

Appendix

But what things were gain to me, these I have counted loss for Christ. Yet indeed I also count all things loss for the excellence of the knowledge of Christ Jesus my Lord, for whom I have suffered the loss of all things, and count them as rubbish, that I may gain Christ and be found in Him, not having my own righteousness, which is from the law, but that which is through faith in Christ, the righteousness which is from God by faith; that I may know Him and the power of His resurrection, and the fellowship of His sufferings, being conformed to His death, if, by any means, I may attain to the resurrection from the dead.
Philippians 3: 7-11

How I Became a Christian

It happened almost fifty years ago. I went to a Lutheran Sunday School as a young child and later faithfully attended a Christian Science Sunday School for the next fourteen years until I went to college. While in high school, one student stood out among his peers because he always carried a big Bible. I tried to avoid him. However, he and I were the only men in my graduating class to be accepted into a special accelerated program at a state university about an hour away. As providence would have it, we became dormitory roommates for two years.

David believed the Bible, including the account of a six-day creation. He was pursuing a degree in Biology and teaching to better defend and communicate his faith. He was an Independent Baptist and wanted to become a pastor. He prayed for me and tried to share his faith. However, I was not too open and preferred to debate with him instead. One day I found a pamphlet on my desk which documented the origins of Christian Science and how its teachings conflicted with the Bible. I read it but wasn't sure how I could win a debate with a pamphlet! However, it did cause me to question the teachings of Christian Science and I became open to the possibility that I was wrong.

My roommate was like a John the Baptist for me. He was sent by God to prepare the way for me to come to Christ. Although it took a couple of years to soften my heart, he did the hard work. He prepared the soil and watered the seed through his life, witness, and prayers. But God used someone else to reap what he had sown.

On a late Friday afternoon in April a friend had invited me to a meeting in a local home where a free home-cooked dinner would be provided. I had planned to head home for the weekend and visit with my parents and family. After waiting over an hour for the Trailways bus, I decided instead to take my friend up on his offer. The opportunity for a free home-cooked meal at a nice home was too much of a temptation for this college dorm student to pass by! I was trying to redeem the evening but God had something much bigger and better in mind.

My friend drove us to the home of the top IBM salesman in the area. It was filled with high-school and college-aged students as it had been on many previous Friday evenings. I was favorably impressed by the friendliness of the people and the hospitality of the host who provided all of the food. After enjoying a nice dinner, I tried to join in as everyone was singing songs about Jesus, accompanied by two guitarists. But I felt out of place like the proverbial bucket under a bull. After the music was over, everyone broke into separate groups.

I joined the other first-timers in a group led by a young man with a very loving and radiant smile. After everyone introduced themselves, he told us a story about a just judge who was also a loving father. He explained how the judge's only son had gotten mixed up with the wrong crowd and was involved in a tragic event that ended in the murder of an innocent person. The trial was to be held by the judge who was unable to recuse himself.

The judge listened attentively as the evidence mounted against his son, pointing to his guilt in a first-degree murder charge. In a heart-wrenching moral dilemma, the judge was torn between his impeccable justice and the deep love he had for his son. Justice demanded the execution of his son but love wanted to find another way. The teacher asked us if anyone had an answer to this tragic dilemma.

After waiting for several minutes with no response, we heard the judge's sentence: "Guilty of murder in the first degree! A life for a life!" Then the judge removed his judicial robe, stepped down from the bench, and presented himself to the bailiff to be taken away. His love and justice would both be satisfied as he surrendered himself to be executed for the murder his son had committed.

The young man with the radiant smile then explained that this was exactly what God had done by sending His Son to die for us. Jesus's death satisfied God's love and justice and made it possible for us to be reconciled to Him. He then gave another example. He took out his wallet and said, "Let this wallet represent your sin." After setting it down, he clasped his two hands together in an interlocking oneness and said, "This represents the original relationship and fellowship God had with man." He then pulled one hand away from the other and clenched it into a fist as he explained how man rebelled against God. He then placed his wallet in the hand that had pulled away as he explained how our sin separates us from God.

We saw the two hands could not come together because the wallet (our sin) separated them. The teacher then took the wallet from the other hand and set it on the floor as he explained how Jesus took away our sins through His death on the cross. He then explained that Jesus left our sins in the grave as He rose from the dead and demonstrated this as one hand left the wallet on the floor. The teacher then explained how we could be reconciled to God if we acknowledged our sin, were willing to turn from it (repent), and receive Jesus Christ as our Savior and follow Him. He then reached up with the one hand to grasp the other hand which was waiting to receive it. Then the two hands interlocked again as one. He assured us that we would then go to heaven if we received Jesus into our lives (John 3:16; 1 John 5:13). But I had a hard time believing I had a sin problem until I heard the next illustrations.

Suppose someone stole your furniture when you were not at home and got caught after selling the furniture and spending all the money. He then comes before the judge and reasons, "Your honor, I think you should let me off because I passed by dozens of houses and did not steal their furniture. The good I did by not stealing their furniture far outweighs the bad of stealing the furniture from this one house. And this is only my first offense." Suppose the judge accepts his reasoning and lets him off. You would probably be pretty upset but could live with the result because your house was insured.

Now suppose you spent your insurance money and bought a house full of new furniture. Then the same thief comes by and steals all your furniture again, while you are on vacation. He sells it, spends the money, gets caught, and comes before the same judge as before. He tells the judge, "I've passed by hundreds of houses since the last time and did not steal their furniture. The good I did by not stealing their furniture far outweighs the bad I did by stealing the furniture from this one house. And, besides, this is only my second offense!" Suppose the judge accepts his reasoning and, once again, lets him off. By now you would rightfully be ticked off at that judge and think, "This is not justice at all!"

Because your insurance was canceled, you have to empty out your bank account and buy some decent used furniture as you try to get on with your life. While you are visiting some friends for an afternoon, this same thief comes by and steals your furniture again! He sells it, spends all the money, gets caught, and comes before the same judge. He uses the same reasoning as before, explaining that because he passed by thousands of houses without stealing their furniture and this is only his third offense, his good far outweighs the bad. The judge sides with him again and lets him off. By this time you should be furious and demand the impeachment of that judge! You know this isn't justice at all!

The teacher explained how we often use the same reasoning as that furniture thief. We think if the good (in our own eyes) we have done outweighs the bad, God will not punish us for our sin. But this is not justice. We also often think God will be lenient with us and overlook our sin. But the Bible says God will by no means allow the guilty to go unpunished (Exodus 34:7). The Bible also says that the wages of sin is death (Romans 6:23). But what is sin?

The teacher explained there are two kinds of sin. The first is the sin of commission when we do something we shouldn't do. The second is the sin of omission where we fail to do something we should do. The word *sin* comes from an ancient Hebrew term which means *to miss the mark*. It is related to archery when the archer misses the bull's eye and exclaims, "I have sinned!"

Sin also means to fall short of God's standard of moral perfection. It included not just wrong actions but also evil thoughts, rotten attitudes, and unkind words. Through the Scriptures, he showed us that we all sinned and stood guilty before God. ("For all have sinned and come short of the glory of God" (Romans 3:23; KJV). "There is none righteous, no not one" (Romans 3:10b; KJV).) But how many times have we sinned?

Suppose I woke up one morning and stubbed my toe and thought some bad thoughts -- a sin of commission. Then suppose I also said a few choice words to my spouse, blaming her because I stubbed my toe -- another sin of commission. To top it off, I did not have a thankful heart -- a sin of omission. I have already sinned three times before even getting out of my bedroom! Suppose you are much better than me and just sinned three times a day. Multiply that by the number of days in a year and you get over a thousand sins a year. Multiply that by your age and you see what I needed to see: We all have a sin problem.

We have each committed thousands and thousands of sins! There is no way the Just Judge can overlook thousands of sins, especially since He will not even overlook one. These illustrations helped me realize that I was a sinner and needed a savior. I realized I deserved to go to hell but Jesus paid for my sin so I could go to heaven.

APPENDIX

The teacher asked if anyone had any questions. I asked him about the heathen and was given a pamphlet to read that would help answer my question. I took it back to the dorm and read it that night. After thinking about what I had heard and read, the next morning I decided to accept Jesus Christ into my life as my Savior and I started my journey with Him.

I didn't know too much about what it meant to follow Jesus as Lord. I am still learning about that! How about you?

If you don't know the Lord, you have no idea how much God loves you. The Holy Spirit grieves for you but He will not manipulate you. Do you want to know how much the Father loves you? He points to His Son and says, "That's how much I love you!" Do you want to know how much Jesus loves you? He opened His arms as wide as they would go and said, "This much!" Then He died.

We follow in the path of the wise men that sought and honored the King.

CPSIA information can be obtained
at www.ICGtesting.com
Printed in the USA
LVHW050731301219
642043LV00003B/248/P